Demand Forecasting for Inventory Control

Nick T. Thomopoulos

Demand Forecasting for Inventory Control

Springer

Nick T. Thomopoulos
Stuart School of Business
Illinois Institute of Technology
Burr Ridge
Illinois
USA

ISBN 978-3-319-11975-5 ISBN 978-3-319-11976-2 (eBook)
DOI 10.1007/978-3-319-11976-2

Library of Congress Control Number: 2014954807

Springer Cham Heidelberg New York Dordrecht London

Printed on acid-free paper

Springer is part of Springer Science+Business Media (www.springer.com)

For my wife, my children, and my grandchildren

Preface

Looking back over my working years, I was most fortunate with the background gained as it happened to unfold from year-to-year in both industry and in academia. This included working in industry at International Harvester as supervisor of operations research in the corporate headquarters; at IIT Research Institute (IITRI) as a senior scientist serving as a consultant to international industry and government; as a professor in the Industrial Engineering Department at the Illinois Institute of Technology (IIT) and also in the Stuart School of Business at IIT My experience with FIC Inc., a software company, is where I gained knowledge on the software tools needed in industry, as well as the customers' call for user friendly tools. For many of the years, I was privileged to serve as consultant to a wide variety of industries in the United States, Europe and Asia. At IIT, I was fortunate to be assigned an array of courses, gaining a wide breadth with the variety of topics, and with the added knowledge I gained from the students and with every repeat of the course. I also was fortunate to serve as the advisor to 36 bright Ph.D. students as they carried on their dissertation research. Bits of knowledge from the various courses and research helped me in the classroom, in research, and also in my consulting assignments. When I could, I used my industry knowledge in classroom lectures so the students could see how some of the textbook methodologies actually are applied in industry. At the same time, the knowledge I gained from the classroom helped me to formulate and develop solutions to industry applications as they unfolded. The wide variety of experience allowed me to paint a picture on which quantitative tools really are useful in industry. This book is based on this total experience and also includes the demand forecasting methods that I found doable and helpful to industry.

Thanks foremost to my wife, Elaine Thomopoulos, who has encouraged me to write this volume. She inspired and gave consultation very often as the need called. Thanks also to the many people who have helped and inspired me along the way. I can name only a few here. Raida Abuizam (Purdue University—Calumet), Brian Ahearn (Komatsu Dresser), Wayne Bancroft (Walgreens), Owen Baxter (Wolverine World Wide), Fred Bock (IIT Research Institute), Harry Bock (Florsheim Shoe Company), Randy Braun (Komatsu Dresser), Toemchai Bunnag (PTT Public), John Cada (Florsheim Shoe Company), Dan Cahill (International Truck and Engine), Debbie Cernauskas (Benedictine University), Edine Dahel (Monterey Institute),

John DeMotts (International Harvester), Frank Donahue (Navistar), Nick Faklis (Patterson Office Supplies), Jim Gleason (International Harvester), Mark Graham (International Truck and Engine), Scott Halligas (Florsheim Shoe Compnay), Jim Harrington (International Harvester), Willard Huson (Navistar), Dick Ilseman (International Truck and Engine), Marsha Jance (Indiana University—Richmond), Tom Lewis (International Harvester), Carol Lindee (Panduit), Keith Mahal (Navistar), Nick Malham (FIC Inc.), Craig Marasek (Komatsu Dresser), Pricha Pantumsinchai (M-Focus), Ted Prenting (Marist Colllege), Athapol Ruangkanjanases (Chulalongkorn Univeristy), Doloris Santucci (Navistar), Mark Spieglan (FIC Inc.), and Toli Xanthopoulos, (Mercer Investment Consulting).

Contents

Chapter 1
Demand Forecasting for Inventory Control

1.1 Introduction

1.1.1 Demand Forecasting

Management is continually faced with a fast-paced flow of business planning and decision-making situations. A forecast of some type is used as a basis to meet many of these needs, whereby, the more reliable the forecasts, the better the outcome for the planning and decisions. Forecasting has plagued management for centuries, but now, with the advancement in computers, forecasting methods that previously were impossible to explore are currently achievable.

A sound forecasting system is a necessity in the expanding supply change management world, allowing firms to cope with the ever-changing shifts in demands for their products and resources. The common goal is to have the least amount of inventory to satisfy the customers' demands for its products, and at the same time minimize the cost of buying and holding the inventory. A company with an oversupply in inventory incurs undue costs caused by excess storage, stock deterioration and obsolescence of the items. With an undersupply, expediting, bad will and lost sales results. Reliable forecasts are essential for a company to survive and grow.

In manufacturing, management must forecast the future demands for its products to provide for the materials, labor, and capacity to fulfill these needs. These resources are planned and scheduled well before the demands for the products are placed on the firm.

In inventory holding locations, (distribution centers, stores, dealers), forecasts are essential to the inventory control system. Locations hold thousands of items in stock and must anticipate in advance the demands that will occur against each of these items. This is needed to have the proper inventory available to fill the customers' demands as they come in. In distribution centers, the lead-time is typically two or more months and in stores and dealers it is two or more days. Management must plan in advance for how much inventory to have available. With each item in the inventory, forecasts are needed for the months over the planning horizon. The forecast

N. T. Thomopoulos, *Demand Forecasting for Inventory Control*,
DOI 10.1007/978-3-319-11976-2_1

is the catalyst that determines when to buy and how much. In a typical inventory system, the forecasts are revised once a month for each item in every location, and decisions on when and how much to buy is run daily.

Demand forecasting is a term more recently coined to define the forecast of demands for items in stock. The demands are from customers who want to purchase the item for immediate use. A part number, style number, product number, and so forth identifies each item; and the demand is for the item at a particular stocking location. The term stock-keeping-unit (sku) represents an item at a particular location.

1.1.2 At the Beginning

Eli Whitney in 1797 used assembly lines to mass-produce muskets for the US government. All the parts of the musket were produced with the same engineering tolerances so that each could be inserted into any musket. In this way, the parts and components were standard. From that era on, as soon as mass production of items became a reality, and the items were offered for sale to the public, forecasts on the number of future sales of the items was needed to determine how many items to produce over the near planning horizon.

Standard parts were also used in the design of the finished good items. Over time, with customer use, some of the parts wore-out or were damaged in use, and the customers could purchase a replacement part to reinsert in the finished good item. Thereby forecasts were also needed on each replacement part. An extra supply of inventory was needed to provide for the projected replacement needs. The replacement parts are now called service parts.

The forecasting methods of products and replacement parts were limited since data collection and large computations were inaccessible, slow and difficult. It was not common to save the quantity of sales by item over the prior time periods, and computation mechanisms were not available to help in the mathematical manipulations.

1.1.3 Calculators

In the 1800s, a few mechanical calculators that could add and subtract were produced. The face of the machines included rows and columns of buttons to press to insert the numbers. These machines were slightly helpful to the person responsible to forecast future demands of each item. Mechanical calculators became more common in the early 1900s, and by the 1950s they were able to add, subtract, multiple and divide numbers. However, the machines were noisy and wearing on the user.

In the 1960s, battery and electronic handheld calculators became available and some had printing capability. As the prices of these newer calculators became cheaper and their use more popular, the need for mechanical calculators diminished and soon the mechanical units fell out of use in the workplace. Still, those persons responsible to project (forecast) the sales of items were limited to the mathematical functions available (add, subtract, multiply, divide, square root) in the newer electronic calculators.

1.1.4 Data Processing

In the meantime, automatic data processing was starting with the introduction of the punched card system in the late 1880s by Herman Hollerith. The first successful application of this system occurred during the 1890 US Census. Subsequently, the system was oriented for commercial use, and slowly the punched card system improved. By 1928, the card had capacity of 80 columns and 12 rows. A host of machines (card punchers, collators, sorters, interpreters, so on) became available to process the cards for a variety of functions. The punched card allowed the storage of numbers so that the machines could be used to process the numbers in a variety of ways. This capability allowed the forecaster more flexibility in the collection and computations needed to forecast future demands on each item.

Electronic processing grew in the 1950s when magnetic tapes were introduced to store the numbers. The tapes and the cards were used together to process the numbers for all types of commercial companies. The use was for payroll, invoicing, inventory, account receivable and so forth. But as before, the primary mathematical functions of the systems were adding, subtracting, multiplying, and dividing. The people responsible for developing forecasting methods were limited to the capabilities of the machines available to them in that era.

1.1.5 Forecasting Pioneers

Looking back, three individuals (Brown, Holt, Winters) were the pioneers in demand forecasting. They developed forecast models that are still in common use today. All three used a method called exponential smoothing that requires only the demand from the most current time period. In the 1950s, it was not common to store and save multiple time periods of demand.

In 1956, Robert G. Brown was the first to apply the forecasting method called exponential smoothing. The method required the demand from the most recent time period (month, week) and a coefficient from the prior time period. The method is called single exponential smoothing and requires one coefficient (called the level) from the prior time period. The single exponential smoothing method generated forecasts for horizontal demand patterns. The method combines the current demand entry with the past coefficient and is an easy mathematical step to apply, either by data processing or by a hand-held calculator. Brown also introduced a double exponential smoothing model to forecast trend demand patterns, and a triple exponential smoothing model to forecast quadratic demand patterns. The single exponential smoothing model is still in high use today and is described fully in Chap. 3. The trend and quadratic models are not in common use anymore. In the 1970s, the author was privileged to work along with Robert G. Brown on an inventory consulting assignment at a large automotive corporation.

In 1957, Charles C. Holt added a trend component to the exponential smoothing method and this allowed forecasts that included trends up or down. The model requires two coefficients (level and slope). To apply the method, the demand from the most current time period is needed, along with two coefficients from the forecast model. As before, the current demand is smoothed with the prior forecast coefficients. Holt's trend method is still is high use today and is described in Chap. 4.

In 1960, Peter Winters, along with Holt, added seasonal components to the exponential smoothing forecasts. The forecast model requires three coefficients, (level, slope, and seasonal). Two models were introduced, the multiplicative model and the additive model. As in the prior exponential smoothing models, only the demand from the most current time period and three coefficients from the prior time period are needed to generate the forecast. This model is described in Chap. 5.

1.1.6 Computer Era

In the 1940s, computers with many thousands of vacuum tubes were developed, like the ENIAC for government research use. Moving on to the 1950s, computers with transistors became available for use in research facilities.

The author took a graduate course using the then state-of-art ILLIAC computer at the University of Illinois in 1957. The input and output mode to the computer was by way of a five-hole capacity (half-inch wide) paper tape. The programming code was crude and limited in capability. The code was punched onto the paper tape from a separate machine and when completed, the paper tape was inserted in the computer for processing. If the code was without any faults, a paper tape was punched as the output. The output tape was inserted into another machine that printed the output results. The author remembers many agonizing late nights at the computer lab until the homework assignment was successful.

In the 1960s, more commercial friendly computers became available, the IBM 650, IBM 700 series, and later the IBM 1401. Other computer manufacturers included Burroughs, Control Data, Honeywell, Sperry-Rand, so forth. Two basic programming languages became available for use, COBOL (common business oriented language) for commercial use, and FORTRAN (formula translator) for scientific use. From that point on, computer programmers were handed powerful tools that could apply to all sorts of developments in research and industry. Inventory control was now becoming more accessible to companies since demands from the past time periods could readily be stored and used in developing more powerful demand forecasting methods.

1.1.7 Qualification

Demand forecasting can be done using different time periods, e.g., days, weeks, months or quarters. Once the time period is chosen, the demand history for these periods of time in the past are used to project the demands for equal length time periods in the future. The concepts presented in this book can be used for any type of time period. However, to avoid confusion and complexity, the author has chose to write this book using only monthly time periods. Conversion to other time periods is left up to the reader.

1.2 Chapter Summaries

The following is a list of the remaining chapters and a quick summary on the content of each.

Chapter 2. Demand History Forecasts are necessary for each part in every stocking location as they are used in the stocking decisions on when to replenish the stock and how much. The forecasts are typically revised each month as the new monthly demand entry becomes available. The forecasts are based on the history flow of the demands over the past months. The more accurate the demand history, the better the forecasts. The typical inventory system saves anywhere from 12–36 months of demand history.

The data to save is the monthly demand history, denoted as, x(1), …, x(N), where x(t) is the demand in month t, $t=1$, the oldest month in the history, and $t=\mathrm{N}$, the most current month. The demand history to save varies depending on the stock keeping facility. Often, the database history includes the monthly demands and monthly lines, where each customer order represents a line and the quantity on the order is the demand. At the end of each month, the total demands and lines are tallied for the month. The database may also include the demand-to-date for the current month as it is progressing. In service parts distribution centers, the demands from dealers are often classified as either regular or emergency. For distribution centers that supply retail stores, the demands may be labeled as new stock and replenish stock. New stock includes the initial delivery to the stores. Some stocking facilities save their demands on a weekly basis rather than monthly.

Plants often operate with fiscal (rather than calendar) months that are denoted as 445 or 454 or 544. Some distribution centers have demands that are classified as either regular demands and as other-requirements. Other requirements are from out-of-the-ordinary customers. In some distribution centers and stores, the demands may be partitioned as regular demands and as promotion demands. Another type of demand is called advance demand and this occurs when a distribution center receives a customer order that is not to be shipped until some future date. When demands are shipped incorrectly, the customer returns the stock to the stocking location and these are labeled as return demands. Sometimes unusual events occur that cause a spike in the demand, or an error happens in order entry where the quantity or part number enters incorrectly, causing the entry on the database to be significantly different from the normal flow and is called an outlier demand. This type of demand is damaging to the forecasts and needs to be found and adjusted accordingly, prior to the forecasts. The flow of the demands, called the demand pattern, is mostly of the horizontal, trend or seasonal type. The chapter describes a way to convert fractional forecasts to integer forecast; and how to compute cumulative forecasts for the future months. Some statistics from an actual inventory system is presented.

Chapter 3. Horizontal Forecasts Perhaps the most typical demand pattern is the horizontal where the month-to-month demands fluctuate above and below a path (called the level) without any trend or seasonal influence. This chapter describes five horizontal forecasting models. These forecast models are here called the following: horizontal forecast, horizontal moving average forecast, horizontal discount forecast, horizontal smoothing forecast, and forecasts using 2 stages. In all situations, the concept of raw and integer forecasts is shown. For each of the models, monthly raw forecasts are generated in fractional form. A corresponding set of forecasts is called integer forecasts and these are converted from the raw forecasts by way of the rounding algorithm. A key measure of the forecasts is the standard deviation of the one-month forecast errors. This measure is needed subsequently when inventory decision are computed. Another useful measure, the coefficient-of-variation, is a relative way to measure the forecast error.

Chapter 4. Trend Forecasts Some of the items stocked in the inventory have demand patterns where the month-to-month level is gradually increasing (or decreasing) in a steady way, and thereby, a trend forecast model is called. The model has two coefficients, a and b, where a is the intercept and b is the slope. Three such models are described here: trend regression forecasts, trend discount forecasts and trend smoothing forecasts. The trend regression forecast model generates a straight line fit through the most recent N history demands giving equal weight to each history demand. The trend discount forecast model also uses the N most recent history demands, but gives relatively less weight to each older demand. This model is based on a discount parameter, β, that specifies how to apportion the weight to each older demand entry. The trend smoothing forecast model revises the forecast coefficients as each new demand entry becomes available. The model has two parameters, α and β, that are used to revise the trend coefficients, (a, b), at each month. All three of the forecast models generate forecasts that are in fractional numbers and are here called raw forecasts. The forecasts are converted to integers using the cumulative rounding algorithm described in Chap. 2. For latter use, in inventory control, the standard deviation of each of the forecast models is also generated each month. For comparative sake, the coefficient of variation, cov, is also generated each month. Three forecast models are described for dampening the fast declining forecasts.

Chapter 5. Seasonal Forecasts Seasonal forecasts are needed when the demands over a year have a cyclical flow such as the rise for light clothing during the summers; heavy clothing during the winters; school supplies in late summers; antifreeze during the winters; golf balls in the summers; cold tablets in the winters; and sunglasses in the summers. Two forecast models are described: the seasonal smoothing multiplicative forecast model, and the seasonal smoothing additive forecast model. Perhaps the most common application of the model is when the demands are monthly covering 12 months in a year. The seasonal multiplicative model is described fully with example data. The model has two stages: first is to initialize the forecasts using the most current N history demands, and second is to revise the forecasts as each new monthly demand becomes available. The model includes a trend component and twelve seasonal ratios for each month of the year. The trend component could be flat, rising or falling, and the seasonal ratios could vary for each month of the year indicating an increase or decrease in the demands for the month relative to the trend. The model requires three smoothing parameters that assign higher weights to the more recent demands in the history. This way, the forecasts can readily react to any changes in the demand flow of the items in forecast. For brevity, an abridged discussion of the seasonal additive model is presented.

Chapter 6. Promotion Forecasts Promotions come in various ways: price reduction, buy one get one free, zero interest, no money down, and so on. They often occur when a supplier or a stock location offers a price incentive of some sort to the customers to buy now with enticements for purchases in larger quantities. The promotion typically has a start-date and end-date, and the demand during these days is relatively higher than the normal non-promo days. This situation causes wild fluctuations in the demand history and upsets the forecasting model in use. The standard deviation increases and the forecast coefficients swing out of normal control. Special adjustments are needed in the forecast models to overcome the fluctuations. Two forecast models are described here to accommodate the promotion activity: the promotion horizontal model and the promotion trend model. Both of the models involve two stages: the initial stage and the revision stage. The initial stage is the first estimates of the coefficients of the model. This stage requires N history months of demands and promotion measures. The coefficients of the model are estimated using regression methods where equal weight is given to each of the history months. The revision stage is used for the months after the initial stage where the coefficients are revised every month with each current month's data using the smoothing method. The standard deviation and the coefficient of variation are computed for each of the two stages.

Chapter 7. Multi SKU Forecasts An sku is an abbreviation for the term stock-keeping-unit that identifies an item being in the inventory at a stocking location. Could be a part number, a product number, a style number, so forth. Should a model of a certain tool be in stock at a dealer, it is an sku at that dealer. If the same model is in stock in 1000 dealers, it is an sku in each of the 1000 dealers. It is also an sku at each distribution center that stocks the model. A truck parts dealer typically has 15,000 skus and a truck distribution center may have 100,000 skus. A shoe store in the mall may have 2000 skus in shoes alone, since each style by size and width is a separate sku. Forecasts are needed for each sku (usually monthly) to use in the inventory stocking computations.

When a part is stocked as a service part in an inventory system with five distribution centers (DC), the part is an sku in each of the DC's. Forecasts are needed for each part by location to arrange for the proper stock at each location. A forecast is also needed for the aggregate demands of the part in all locations so economic replenishments of the part from the supplier can be determined.

Consider a style shoe with 36 size and width combinations. Each size and width for the style shoe is an sku. Forecasts are needed for each size and width to be used in the inventory decisions at the distribution centers and at each store. The forecast is typically generated for the style itself, and this forecast is apportioned down to each of the size and width combinations. The same scenario also occurs in clothing, like men's shirts, with different sizes, and so forth.

This chapter describes two common ways to forecast when multiple skus are of concern in an inventory system, the top-down method and the bottom-up method. Top-down is when the aggregate demand history is used to forecast the demands over the future months. The aggregate forecast is then allocated down to each sku using an sku percent representing it's portion of the total demand. This way, the forecasts for the total and for each sku are generated in a systematic manner. The bottom-up method is in use when a forecast is generated for each sku and the sum of the sku forecasts are used to determine the forecast for the total.

In both methods, the standard deviation of each forecast is of need for subsequent use in inventory decisions. Methods are shown on how to compute the standard deviations for each sku and for the total when the top-down and bottom-up methods are in use.

Chapter 8. Forecast Sensitivity Along the supply chain, in distribution centers, stores, dealers, so forth, forecasts are in continual need for inventory decisions to project the flow of demands over the future months for each item stocked. The more accurate the forecasts, the better the inventory decisions and the more profitable the entity. A 10 % decrease in the measure of the forecast error will result in approximately a 10 + percent decrease in the amount of safety stock needed. This reduced stock is very helpful to the profit margin on the inventory system.

In this chapter, a series of simulation runs are developed to apprise the forecaster on how some elements in forecasting affect the accuracy of the forecasts. For this purpose, the forecast accuracy is measured by the coefficient of variation, cov, of the one-month ahead forecast error. A first series of tests concern the number of months of demand history to use in developing the forecasts. The cov is measured as the history of demands range from 6 to 48 months and the forecasts are for the horizontal and trend demand patterns. A second series of tests are aimed at measuring how forecast accuracy depends on the choice of parameters and forecast model selected. Three separate simulations are run; one for the horizontal demand pattern, another for the trend demand pattern, and yet another for the seasonal demand pattern. A third series of tests demonstrate how damaging outlier demands are to the forecasts and the forecast accuracy. Two examples are given, one for a horizontal demand pattern and another for a trend demand pattern.

Chapter 9. Filtering Outliers A primary goal of forecasting is to measure the flow of demands from the history months and project to the future months with a minimum forecast error. A way to enhance this goal is by filtering the history demands to seek out any outlier demands and adjust accordingly. As demonstrated in the prior chapter, outlier demands cause much damage to the forecasts and increase the forecast error. Filtering of the demand history is not an easy process, but is important to yield forecasts with minimal forecast error. Reducing the forecast error will reduce the amount of safety stock needed to run the inventory operation. This chapter shows a way to seek out and adjust any outlier demands from the history months when the demand patterns are of the horizontal, trend or seasonal type. The filtering process takes place just prior to generating the forecasts.

Another way to minimize outlier demands is by filtering the line demands that occur in the order entry phase of the inventory stocking location. This is when the customers send in the purchase orders and list on each line of the order, a part number and a quantity. This part number request is a line demand and can be filtered to seek if it is an outlier. If an outlier is detected here, the line demand is sent back to the customer seeking verification on the quantity.

Chapter 10. Standard Normal and Truncated Normal Distributions The normal distribution is perhaps the most commonly used probability distribution in materials management as well as in many other scientific developments. This chapter shows how the variable x, from the normal, is related to the standard normal distribution with variable z. A portion of the standard normal contains all values of (z>k) where k is a specific value of z. Of particular interest in subsequent use is the partial mean and partial standard deviation of the measure (z-k) from this portion of the standard normal. Another useful distribution is the truncated normal that also is defined with a parameter k. This distribution has many shapes and a measure of interest is the coefficient of variation, cov, that helps to identify the shape of the distribution. The two distributions, standard normal and truncated normal, have applications in inventory control and examples on how they are used appears in Chaps. 11 and 12.

Chapter 11. Safety Stock Safety stock is the extra inventory to hold for an item for protection against demands exceeding the forecast. This type of stock concerns entities where the demands of the future are not known until they happen, like in distribution centers, stores and dealers. In plants, where the production schedules are set in advance, safety stock is usually not needed. The typical way to measure the variability in the forecasts is by the one month ahead forecast error. A relative measure is the coefficient of variation. Two common methods of generating the safety stock are: the service level (probability not out of stock), and the percent fill (ratio of demand filled over total demand) methods. Both methods are also sometimes referred as the service level method. The normal distribution is used primarily to generate how much safety stock to have available. This chapter shows how the truncated normal distribution can also serve this function. The truncated normal has many shapes and includes only portions of the right-hand-side of the standard normal.

Chapter 12. Auxiliary Forecasts Management often needs forecasts that are not like the models described in the earlier chapters that are generated using the flow of demands from the history months. This chapter describes some of the more commonly needed forecasts of this type. A first concerns the forecasts for the first future month and the demand-to-date as the month is progressing. For the first month, a forecast has already been generated, and as the month progresses, the demand-to-date demand is evolving. The forecast for the remaining portion of the month is generated along with the associated standard deviation. Another scenario occurs for parts when some demands are ordered for future deliveries, called advance demands. A forecast for the future month has already been generated in the usual way from the flow of history demands. An adjustment to the future month's forecast is developed based on the advance demand information. Another situation that often occurs in service parts inventory is when a forecast is needed on a part even when no history demands are available. This happens when a new part is included on the bill-of-material of a finished good item due to an engineering change or a redesign, and the part is to be immediately held in inventory at the service part location. This situation is called the initial buy quantity. Another condition that takes place often in service parts locations is when the supplier will stop supplying the part, even when the service part location is obliged to carry the part for future possible needs from its customers. This is called the all-time-buy.

Chapter 2
Demand History

2.1 Introduction

Forecasts are necessary for each part in every stocking location as they are used in the stocking decisions on when to replenish the stock and how much. The forecasts are typically revised each month as the new monthly demand entry becomes available. The forecasts are based on the history flow of the demands over the past months. The more accurate the demand history, the better the forecasts. The typical inventory system saves anywhere from 12 to 36 months of demand history.

The data to save is the monthly demand history, denoted as, x(1),…, x(N), where x(t) is the demand in month t, t = 1, the oldest month in the history, and t = N, the most current month. The demand history to save varies depending on the stock keeping facility. Often, the database history includes the monthly demands and monthly lines, where each customer order represents a line and the quantity on the order is the demand. At the end of each month, the total demands and lines are tallied for the month. The database may also include the demand-to-date for the current month as it is progressing. In service parts distribution centers, the demands from dealers are often classified as either regular or emergency. For distribution centers that supply retail stores, the demands may be labeled as new stock and replenish stock. New stock includes the initial delivery to the stores. Some stocking facilities save their demands on a weekly basis rather than monthly. Plants often operate with fiscal (rather than calendar) months that are denoted as 445 or 454 or 544.

Some distribution centers have demands that are classified as either regular demands and as other-requirements. Other requirements are from out-of-the-ordinary customers. In some distribution centers and stores, the demands may be partitioned as regular demands and as promotion demands. Another type of demand is called advance demand and this occurs when a distribution center receives a customer order that is not to be shipped until some future date. When demands are shipped incorrectly, the customer returns the stock to the stocking location and these are labeled as return demands. Sometimes unusual events occur that cause a spike in the demand, or an error happens in order entry where the quantity or part number enters incorrectly, causing the entry on the database to be significantly different from the normal flow

N. T. Thomopoulos, *Demand Forecasting for Inventory Control*,
DOI 10.1007/978-3-319-11976-2_2

and is called an outlier demand. This type of demand is damaging to the forecasts and needs to be found and adjusted accordingly, prior to the forecasts. The flow of the demands, called the demand pattern, is mostly of the horizontal, trend or seasonal type. The chapter describes a way to convert fractional forecasts to integer forecasts; and how to compute cumulative forecasts for the future months. An inventory profile section is given that summarizes some revealing statistics on the demand history and forecast results that are taken from an actual large inventory holding system.

2.2 Customer Demand History for a Part

The demand history (for a part) is the main data used to generate a forecast for the future months. The history of customer demands is usually denoted as: x(1), …, x(N) where x(t) is the demand in month t. For newer parts, *N* is also the number of months of history since the part was introduced. For long time parts, *N* may be cut off to 12, or 24 or 36 months depending on the discretion of the management. The number of lines for month t, n(t), is also useful information and the history is here denoted as: n(1),…, n(N). Using the history of the demands and of the lines, it is possible to compute the history of pieces-per-line and this is denoted as: d'(1), …, d'(N) where d'(t) = 0 if n(t) = 0, otherwise, d'(t) = x(t)/n(t). Note also, the number of pieces for line i in month t is here denoted as: $d_{(i, t)}$ i = 1, …, n(t). The corresponding demands for month t is tallied from: $x(t) = d_{(1,t)} + \ldots + d_{(n(t),t)}$.

In summary, the notation on the demand history of a part is denoted as follows:

N = number of months history saved
t = 1,…, N = demand history months
x(t) = demands in month t
n(t) = number of lines in month t
d'(t) = x(t) / n(t) = pieces-per-line in month t

2.3 Demand-to-Date

Another piece of demand data that may become useful occurs in the first future month of forecasts as time rolls on. This is the month immediately after month t = N that has been previously labeled as the last month of the history months. In month N + 1, the first subsequent month after t = N, the demands to date for a part, are here labeled as x_w, and the corresponding portion of time of this month, is labeled as *w*. This data is dynamic. the entry x_w will change with each new demand in the month, and *w* will change with each day of the month. This data is useful to determine the integrity of the month-1 forecast, as the month progresses.

A summary of the data for the current month to date is below:

x_w = demand for current-month-to-date
w = portion of current month-to-date ($0 \leq w \leq 1$)

2.4 Service Part Regular and Emergency Demands

In a service parts distribution center, DC, of finished goods items (autos, trucks, farm equipment, construction equipment) the DC carries service parts to fill the demands that come from its dealers. The demands are of two type, regular and emergency. When a customer orders with a regular line, this is generally to provide stock needed for a subsequent need as it may occur at the dealership, whereas, the quantity on an emergency line is needed to immediately maintain or repair a finished-good-item that is in the dealership in a down status. Typically, the average number of pieces per line for a regular line is larger than for an emergency line.

Some of the data that is useful in this situation is listed below:

x(t) = monthly service part demands from customers
xr(t) = regular service part demands from customers
xe(t) = emergency service part demands from customers

$$x(t) = xr(t) + xe(t)$$

p(r) = probability a line is regular demand
p(e) = probability a line is an emergency demand

$$p(r) + p(e) = 1$$

nr(t) = number of regular lines in month t
ne(t) = number of emergency lines in month t
$n(t) = nr(t) + ne(t)$ = number of lines in month t
$dr_{(i,\,t)}$ = number of pieces for i-th regular demand in month t
$de_{(i,\,t)}$ = number of pieces for i-th emergency demand in month t
dr` = average of regular pieces per line
de` = average of emergency pieces per line
$x(t) = \left[dr_{(1,t)} + \ldots + dr_{(nr(t),t)}\right] + \left[de_{(1,t)} + \ldots + de_{(ne(t),t)}\right]$ = demands for month t

2.5 New and Replenish Stock Demands for Retail Items at DC

Consider a distribution center, DC, for finished-good-items that supplies the stock to retail stores. This could be for shoes, sweaters, furniture, and so on. The sales-person for the DC may visit the stores in his/her territory and arrange to provide a quantity of stock to be stocked for sale for the store customers to view and purchase. This stock is not a true demand at this point, but is here called a new stock demand. Subsequently, should sufficient sales of the item be sold to the store customers, the store may reorder more stock from the DC. This new line of demands is here called replenish stock demands. The initial new stock demand is not really a demand until the customer sends in an order to the DC for replenish stock on the item. In the event the store cannot sell the new stock, the store might return part or all of the new stock that it was initially provided by the DC.

Below is a summary of the data for the supplier of this scenario:

xn(t) = new stock demand at month t
xr(t) = replenish stock demand at month t
$x(t) = xn(t) + xr(t)$ = total demand at month t

2.6 Weekly Demands

Most plants and many retailers operate on a weekly basis and thereby cumulate their requirements and demands weekly. The plants typically schedule their production activities weekly and thereby plan accordingly. Many retail stores also schedule their replenish and promotion plans on a weekly basis. Weekly demands tend to fluctuate more than the counterpart monthly demands, and thereby subsequent weekly forecasts are less accurate than monthly forecasts. Weekly demands also are more compatible to horizontal and trend forecast models, whereas, monthly demands are compatible to horizontal, trend and seasonal forecast models.

Some of the data notation for weekly demands is listed below:

w(t) = demand at week t
Nm = 12 = number months in a year
Nw = 52 = number weeks in a year
Nw/Nm = 4.33 = average weeks in a month
w` = forecast for an average week's demand

if w` is the forecast:

x` = 4.33w` = forecast for an average month
σ_w^2 = variance of weekly demands
$\sigma_x^2 = 4.33\sigma_w^2$ = relation between variance for monthly and weekly demands
$\sigma_x = \sqrt{4.33}\sigma_w = 2.08\sigma_w$ = standard deviation for monthly demands
$\sigma_w = 1/2.08\sigma_x = 0.481\sigma_x$ = standard deviation for weekly demands

If x` is the monthly forecast:

w` = (1/4.33)x` = forecast for an average week

2.7 445 Fiscal Months at Plants

Many plants operate on a fiscal monthly basis of the 445 type. This is when the first three fiscal months of the year are defined as follows: the first four weeks of the year represent fiscal January, the next four weeks are fiscal February, and the next five weeks are fiscal March. The pattern repeats for the remaining nine fiscal months of the year. The fiscal months may also be defined as 454 instead of 445, or by 544 instead of 445. In either case of 454 or 544, the fiscal months are defined by the stated number of weeks in the month. This way of defining the fiscal months ensures that there are twelve fiscal months in a year, and also satisfies the plant's desire to end each fiscal month on the same day of the week, e.g. Saturday.

In summary, the months of the year can be of the calendar type or of the fiscal type as described above. The three options for fiscal months are defined as below.

445 is for fiscal January, February and March.
454 is for fiscal January, February and March.
544 is for fiscal January, February and March.

The pattern is repeated for the remaining 9 months of the year

2.8 Regular Demands and Other Requirements at DCs

A distribution center of service parts is structured to house inventory for its regular customers (dealers) so that the stock is available when the customers send in their orders. The demand history is the data that is used to generate the DC forecasts covering the future months of demands. The forecasts are the tools that allow the DC to properly provide stock for the customers accordingly. On some occasions, usually infrequently, an order will come in from a non-regular customer for one or for a variety of parts. This non-regular customer could be from an overseas location, or a government facility or the military. In any event, the demand is not from the regular set of customers that the forecast covers. It also is often a demand for a future time period, perhaps to be delivered in a future month from the date of the order. This demand is here called an: *other requirement*. The demand is not included in the history of demands that are used to forecast the demands of the regular type demands. The demand is added to the forecasts for the future months and becomes part of the total requirements for the part. The inventory replenishment side of the computations needs to provide stock to cover the forecast of regular demands and also for the other requirements.

Below is a summary of the data described for this scenario.

$x(t)$ = regular demands at t
$xo(t)$ = other requirements at t
$r(t) = x(t) + xo(t)$ = total requirements at t
$x(t)$ t = 1 to N is used to forecast the demands from the regular customers for the future months
$xo(\tau)$ = other requirement for future month τ and is any demand from a non-regular customer base (overseas customer, military order, etc.)

2.9 Regular and Promotion Demands at DCs and Stores

Promotions of various type occur from time to time at the DC or at the dealers. A common promotion is when the supplier offers a discount on the price for all units sold from day d1 to day d2. This could be for one item or for a line of items. The units sold during the promotion period are recorded and identified as promotion demands. The portion of the months that are included in the promotion period could also be recorded. This data is useful in generating forecasts for the future months, when there is no promotion and when there is a promotion.

One way to capture the demands associated with a promotion is as follows. Let p(t) = portion of month t where a promotion is active. If the promotion runs from d1 = June 14 to d2 = July 14, and June is month t = 6, p(6) = (30-13)/30 = 0.57; and p(7) = 14/31 = 0.45. In any month t with no promotion, p(t) = 0. Further, the demands during the promotion period are saved as xp(6) for June, and xp(7) for July. Subsequent computations allow the forecaster to use this data in generating the forecasts.

A review of the data when promotions are involved is listed below:

p(t) = portion of month t when a promotion is live
xr(t) = regular demands at t
xp(t) = promotion demands at t
$x(t) = xr(t) + xp(t)$ = total demands at t

2.10 Advance Demands

On some occasions, a customer places an order for stock to be delivered in a future date, usually a month or two in the future. This demand is not for the current month and thereby is not recorded as a demand in the current month. Instead, the demand is labeled as *advance demand*, for the future month as the order calls. This advance demand is important information and could be used to adjust the forecast for the named future month.

The data (quantity and month) recorded for this demand is the following:
xa(τ) = advance demand for τ-th future month

2.11 Demand Patterns

There are three basic demand patterns: horizontal, trend and seasonal. Horizontal occurs when the demands are neither rising of falling over time whereby the average is relatively steady. Trend is when the demands are gradually increasing or are decreasing over time. Seasonal is when the demands vary by the months of the year, and the pattern repeats every year. Two versions of the seasonal pattern occur: seasonal multiplicative and seasonal additive. Often, low volume parts are of the horizontal type. Mid to high volume parts could follow any of the three demand patterns.

Letting $\mu(t)$represent the average demand at month t, the demand patterns could be defined as follows:

Horizontal

$$\mu(t) = a \qquad a = \text{level}$$

Trend

$$\mu(t) = a + bt \qquad b = \text{slope}$$

Seasonal multiplicative:

$$\mu(t) = (a + bt)r(t)$$

r(t) = seasonal ratio at month t
r(t) = 1 when month t demand is same as the trend (a + bt)
r(t) > 1 = when month t demand is higher than the trend
r(t) < 1 = when month t demand is lower than the trend

Seasonal additive:

$$\mu(t) = (a + bt) + d(t)$$

d(t) = seasonal increment at month t
d(t)=0 = when month t demand is same as the trend
d(t)>0 = when month t demand is higher than the trend
d(t)<0 = when month t demand is lower that the trend

2.12 Return Demands

As an order comes in to a stocking facility with a line of items, each line lists the part and the quantity to ship to the customer. Should an error occur by incorrectly picking the part, in typing the part number or the quantity, the part and quantity are nevertheless shipped to the customer. When the customer discovers the fault, the pieces are returned to the supplier and are here called *returned demands*. The demand history is in error for the part when this event occurs, and a correction to the demand history should be made accordingly.

Suppose the data associated with a returned demand is the following: $xr(t_o)$ = stock returned at month t_o. With this data in hand, a routine is needed to estimate where this demand came from. One possibility is to scan the demand history of the part, $x(1), \ldots, x(N)$ and find the most recent month, t_1, where $x(t_1) \geq xr(t_o)$ and where $t_1 \leq t_o$, and then adjust the demand entry at t_1 as: $x(t_1) = x(t_1) - xr(t_o)$.

2.13 Outlier Demands

On occasion, the demand history may include a demand entry that is significantly beyond the flow of the normal demands in the history. This demand is here called and *outlier demand.* Outlier demands are mostly above the normal flow of demands. An outlier demand could occur in several ways, one is when the demand is ordered for a wrong part, or the quantity ordered is mistyped. This could also occur due to unusual weather conditions, e.g., windshield wiper demands when an unusual ice storm occurs. Outlier demands are very damaging to the accuracy of the forecasts and as much as possible, prior to generating the forecasts, they should be detected and adjusted accordingly.

A routine is needed to seek if any demand entry, say $x(t_o)$, in the history of demands, x(1),…, x(N), is significantly outside the flow of its neighbor demands. Should a demand entry be found, the entry is adjusted accordingly, ideally to fall in line with the flow of all the demand entries.

2.14 Coefficient of Variation

The coefficient of variation, cov, is a relative way to measure the forecast error associated with a part. This is computed by $cov=(\sigma/a)$, where a is the level, and σ is the standard deviation of the one period ahead forecast error. The level, a, is a measure used in forecasting to represent the average flow of demands in the most current month. When a seasonal demand pattern is in effect, the level represents a measure of the seasonally adjusted demand for the current month. The cov is always positive, and the closer to zero, the more accurate the forecasts.

2.15 Demand Distribution

It is possible to estimate the probability distribution of the forecast errors associated with each part. The one month ahead forecast error for month t would be: $e=(x`-x)$ where x` is the forecast of the month's demand and x is the actual demand. The shape of the probability distribution is important in the subsequent computations where the inventory control on the part takes place, when determining the safety stock that complies with the desired service level specified by the management.

Recall, the level, a, represents the average flow of demands at the current time, and σ is the standard deviation of the one month forecast error. Further, $cov=\sigma/a$ is a relative measure of the forecast error on the part. In the event the forecast errors are shaped like a normal distribution, cov is near or less than 0.33. In the event cov is close to 1.00 or above, the distribution is called lumpy and is more like an exponential distribution, which is far different than a normal distribution.

Very often in forecasting, the cov on a part is not in the neighborhood of 0.33, but is much higher. This is especially true on parts where the demands are of the low volume type. The inventory management is here cautioned not to always assume the normal distribution in the inventory analysis for the parts where the cov is relatively high.

2.16 Cumulative Round Algorithm

The demand forecasting models of this book will generate forecasts that are in fractional form, and are here called raw forecasts. The typical inventory system will convert these fractional forecast to integers. A way to do this is introduced below in pseudo code and is called the *cumulative round algorithm* (CRA). The notation uses f(τ) as the raw forecast for future monthτ (τ = 1 to N`) where N` is the number of future months, and x`(τ) is the associated integer forecast.

```
Start
d = 0
for τ = 1 to N`
x`( τ) = integer[f(t) + d + 0.5]
d = d + [f(τ)- x`( τ)]
next τ
End
```

2.17 Cumulative Forecasts

Often, forecasts are needed for an accumulation of future months. If the monthly forecast is denoted as x`(τ) for future month τ, and the cumulative forecast for T future months is X`(T), the computations are as below.

$$\text{If} \quad T = 3, \quad X`(3) = x`(1) + x`(2) + x`(3)$$

$$\text{If} \quad T = 1.7, \quad X`(1.7) = x`(1) + 0.7x`(2)$$

$$\text{If} \quad T = 0.6, \quad X`(0.6) = 0.6x`(1)$$

and so forth.

2.18 Inventory Profile

In this section are some statistics from the service parts division of a large automotive corporation with over 100,000 part numbers and annual demand over $ 1 billion. The service part division includes multiple locations in North America.

Table 2.1 lists the percent of part numbers (%*N*), by number-months-of-demand-history (NMH). Note, 7.0% of the part numbers have 1–12 months of demand

Table 2.1 Percent of part numbers (%*N*), by number-months-of-demand-history (NMH)

NMH	%*N*
1–12	7.0
13–24	6.7
35–36	8.5
37+	77.8
Sum	100

Table 2.2 Percent of part numbers (%*N*), by outlier type (none, low, high)

Outlier Type	%*N*
none	74.7
low	0.1
high	25.2
Sum	100

Table 2.3 Percent of part numbers (%*N*) and percent of annual demand dollars (%$), by forecast type (horizontal, trend, seasonal)

Forecast Type	%*N*	%$
horizontal	52	4
trend	44	69
seasonal	4	27
Sum	100	100

history, while 77.8% have over 36 months of demand history. Note, the system generates roughly 7% of new parts each year; and assuming equilibrium, about 7% of the parts are discarded each year as well. The database holds the most current 36 months of demand history on each part number.

Table 2.2 gives the results of the outlier filtering algorithm, where 74.7% of the part numbers (%*N*) had no outlier detected, 0.1% had a low outlier detected, and 25.2% had a high outlier detected. The filtering process checks all 36 months of demand history in each of the distribution centers. Each of the 36 demands are checked in every distribution center and should any be significantly out-of-the-ordinary, the part is labeled as an outlier.

Table 2.3 lists the type of forecast model by percent of part numbers (%*N*), and percent of annual demand in dollars (%$). The table shows where 52% of the part numbers had a horizontal forecast model and this amounted to 4% of the annual demands in dollars. Note also where 4% of part numbers have a seasonal forecast model and they amount to 27% of the annual demands in dollars.

Table 2.4 gives the monthly growth rate, g, of the part numbers, by percent of part numbers, (%*N*), and percent of annual demand in dollars, (%$). The monthly growth rate was computed by: $g=(a+b)/a$ where a is the level and b is the slope. Note, 74% of the part numbers had a monthly growth rate of (0.995–1.005) and these parts amounted to 36% of the annual demands in dollars.

Table 2.5 gives the monthly coefficient of variation, cov, by percent of part numbers (%*N*), and percent of annual demand dollars (%$). The table shows where 26%

Table 2.4 Percent of part numbers (%*N*), and percent of annual demand dollars (%$), by monthly growth rate (g)

Growth Rate	%*N*	%$
1.030–	1	3
1.005–1.030	14	29
0.995–1.005	74	36
0.970–0.995	10	30
–0.970	1	2
Sum	100	100

Table 2.5 Percent of part numbers (%*N*), and percent of annual demand dollars (%$), by 1-month coefficient of variation (COV)

COV	%*N*	%$
0.0–0.3	26	68
0.3–0.5	12	16
0.5–0.8	12	7
0.8–1.0	10	4
1.0–	40	5
Sum	100	100

of the part numbers had a cov of (0.0–0.3) and these amounted to 68 % of the annual demand in dollars. Note, 50 % of the parts have irregular (lumpy) demands since the cov is 0.80 or larger. But these parts are a combination of low volume and low value since they amount to only 9 % of the annual dollar demand. 84 % of the annual dollar demands are from parts with a cov of 0.5 or less.

Summary

The more precise and detailed the demand history on each part in the stocking location, the more flexibility and accurate the forecasts become. In the typical stocking location, the demand history is saved in calendar monthly or weekly buckets. Plants often save their demands in fiscal 445 type monthly buckets. One or more years of demand history is needed to generate the forecasts. Various type of demands are saved, depending on the operation of the stocking location. The various type of demand include the following: regular, emergency, advance stock, regular stock, promotion, other-requirements, new stock, advance demands and return demands. In some stocking locations, the history of the number of customer lines is saved and becomes useful in generating the forecasts. Sometimes outlier demands creep into the demand history and it is important to seek out and adjust the outliers accordingly. The more accurate demands, the better the forecasts. Care in the forecasts is essential, since good forecasts will minimize the events of lost sales, backorders and surplus. The coefficient of variation, cov, is a useful relative measure on the forecast accuracy of a part. Also described is the cumulative round algorithm that converts fractional forecasts into integer forecasts. Also of occasional need are cumulative forecasts for various durations of the future months.

Chapter 3
Horizontal Forecasts

3.1 Introduction

Perhaps the most typical demand pattern is the horizontal where the month-to-month demands fluctuate above and below a path (called the level) without any trend or seasonal influence. This chapter describes five horizontal forecasting models. These forecast models are here called the following: horizontal forecast, horizontal moving average forecast, horizontal discount forecast, horizontal smoothing forecast, and forecasts using 2 stages. In all situations, the concept of raw and integer forecasts is shown. For each of the models, monthly raw forecasts are generated in fractional form. A corresponding set of forecasts is called integer forecasts and these are converted from the raw forecasts by way of the rounding algorithm. A key measure of the forecasts is the standard deviation of the 1-month forecast errors. This measure is needed subsequently when inventory decision are computed. Another useful measure, the coefficient-of-variation, is a relative way to measure the forecast error.

3.2 Horizontal Forecasts

When the least square method is used to generate a horizontal forecast model, a parameter N specifies the number of history demands to use in the forecast. The most recent N demands are denoted as x(1), …, x(N) where x(t) is the demand in month t, t = 1 is the oldest month, and t = N is the most recent month. The forecast for the τ-th future month is

$$f(\tau) = a \qquad \tau = 1, 2, \ldots$$

where a is called the level representing the average demand per month.

N. T. Thomopoulos, *Demand Forecasting for Inventory Control*,
DOI 10.1007/978-3-319-11976-2_3

The estimate of the level is obtained by formulating the expression on the sum of squares, S(e), as below,

$$S(e) = \Sigma_{t=1}^{N}\left[x(t) - a\right]^2$$

where e(t) = [x(t) − a] is the residual error at history month t. The value of the level, a, that yields the minimum of S(e) is called the least squares estimate, and in this situation, the level becomes,

$$a` = \Sigma_{t=1}^{N} x(t)/N$$

3.3 Raw Forecasts

The forecasts for the τ-th future month is thereby,

$$f(\tau) = a` \qquad \tau = 1, 2, \ldots$$

This forecast is here called a raw forecast since the forecast values are most likely fractions, same as the value of a`.

3.4 Cumulative Rounding Algorithm

In most systems, the raw forecasts, f(τ), are converted to integer forecasts, denoted as x`(τ). Various ways to do this are in use. A cumulative-rounding algorithm (CRA) to accomplish is described below in a pseudo code manner. The method assumes N` future forecasts are needed.

```
Start
d = 0
For τ = 1 to N'
x'(τ) = integer[f(τ) + d + 0.5]
d = d + [f(τ) - x`( τ)]
next τ
End
```

The algorithm applies for any of the forecast models presented subsequently in this book for the purpose of converting the raw forecasts, f(τ), to integer forecasts, x`(τ).

Example 3.1 Suppose a part is to be forecast with the horizontal forecast model and the forecast parameter is $N = 12$. Assume the most recent 12 demands are the following: 10, 12, 6, 9, 4, 10, 6, 7, 9, 8, 13, 11. Below shows how to find the estimate of the level, and generate the raw and integer forecasts for the future months. The example further describes how to estimate the standard deviation of the forecast error and compute the associated coefficient of variation.

3.5 Estimate the Level

Using the least squares method, the estimate of the level is obtained by seeking the minimum sum of square of errors as shown below:

The residual error for month t, here denoted as e(t), is obtained from, e(t) = (x(t) − a`). The associated sum of square of residual errors, referred as S(e), is the following:

$$S(e) = \Sigma_{t=1}^{N} (e(t))^2$$

Using calculus, the value of the level that minimizes S(e) is obtained, thus yielding the least sum of square errors. The optimal value of the level becomes

$$a` = \Sigma_{t=1}^{N} x(t)/N$$

Since, $\Sigma_{t=1}^{N} x(t) = 105$ and $N = 12$, the estimated of the level is:

$$a` = 105/12 = 8.75$$

3.6 Raw Forecasts

The raw forecast for the τ-th future month is simply,

$$f(\tau) = a` = 8.75 \qquad \tau = 1, 2, \ldots\ldots$$

3.7 Integer Forecasts

To convert the raw forecasts to integer forecasts, the algorithm listed earlier is now demonstrated where the associated integer forecasts are denoted as x`(τ) for τ = 1, 2, … Table 3.1 is a worksheet that shows how to convert the raw forecasts, f(τ), to integer forecasts, x`(τ) for each of the future months, τ = 1 to 12. To begin, d is set to zero. At each τ, the raw forecast becomes the integer of [f(τ) + d + 0.5]. The entry, d is then revised by d = d + [f(τ) − x`(τ)].

Figure 3.1 is a plot of the 12 history demands, followed by the 12 future integer forecasts.

Table 3.1 Worksheet to convert raw forecasts, f(τ), to integer forecasts x`(τ) for Example 3.1

τ	f(τ)	d	[f(τ)+d+0.5]	x`(τ)	d+[f(τ)−x`(τ)]
1	8.75	0.00	9.25	9	−0.25
2	8.75	−0.25	9.00	9	−0.50
3	8.75	−0.50	8.75	8	0.25
4	8.75	0.25	9.50	9	0.00
5	8.75	0.00	9.25	9	−0.25
6	8.75	−0.25	9.00	9	−0.50
7	8.75	−0.50	8.75	8	0.25
8	8.75	0.25	9.50	9	0.00
9	8.75	0.00	9.25	9	−0.25
10	8.75	−0.25	9.00	9	−0.50
11	8.75	−0.50	8.75	8	0.25
12	8.75	0.25	9.50	9	0.00

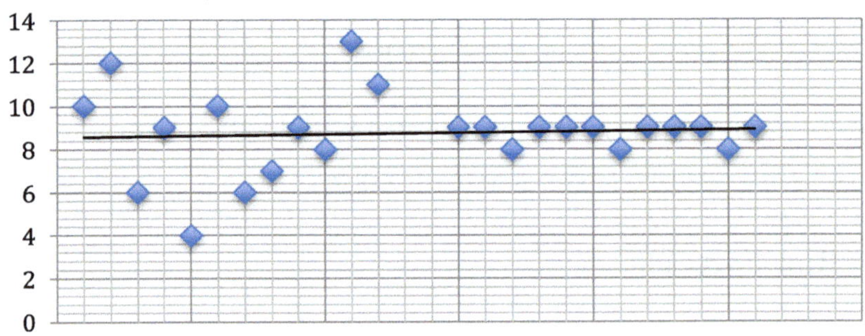

Fig. 3.1 Plot of the history demands and the forecasts for Example 3.1

3.8 Standard Deviation and Cov

The computations to find the estimate of the standard deviation of the forecast errors, and also the corresponding coefficient of variation are now described. The estimate of the standard deviation, denoted here as s, is obtained from the sum of square of errors, S(e), as follows:

$$
\begin{aligned}
s &= \sqrt{S(e)/(N-1)} \\
&= \sqrt{78.419/(12-1)} \\
&= \sqrt{7.129} \\
&= 2.67
\end{aligned}
$$

Finally, the coefficient of variation is obtained as below:

$$cov = s/a` = 2.67/8.75 = 0.305$$

3.9 Horizontal Moving Average Forecasts

The horizontal moving average forecast model is associated with a parameter, N, that specifies the number of months history to use in calculating the average. The average is from the most recent N demand entries, x(1), …, X(N), where N is the most recent demand. In forecasting, the average is called the level and is labeled as a. For this forecast model, the estimate of the level becomes,

$$a` = [x(1) + \ldots + x\ (N)]/N$$

A difficulty occurs for new parts where the number of months of history (nmh) is smaller than the parameter, N. This is overcome by using the following temporary parameter, N` as below:

$$N` = Min(N, nmh)$$

Example 3.2 Suppose a forecaster wants to use the horizontal moving average model with parameter N=10. To begin, the only history demand is at nmh=1, where x(1)=10. Applying the rule given above, the temporary parameter becomes, N`=1, and thereby the estimate of the level is a`=x(1)=10.00. Suppose at nmh=2, x(2)=12, thereby N`=2, and a`=[10+12]/2=11.00. Also assume at nmh=3, x(3)=6, yielding N`=3, and a`=[10+12+6]=9.33. Table 3.2, lists the demands, x(t), for the first 12 months of history for the part, along with the parameter to use, N`, and the estimate of the level, a`, that results. Figure 3.2 depicts the estimated values of the level for the first 12 months of history.

Table 3.3 is a snapshot of the raw and integer forecasts over the next 12 months for the part when the number of months of history is nmh=12. Note from Table 3.2, the 10 month moving average of the demands is a`=8.30. So, the raw forecasts for each of the future months is f(τ)=8.30. The corresponding integer forecasts, x`(τ), are listed in the table.

3.10 Standard Deviation and Cov

The standard deviation of the forecast errors is estimated in the same way as the earlier horizontal (least squares) forecast. In this situation, the most recent N` demand entries are computed. When (nmh<N), all the past history months are used, but when (nmh ≥ N), only the most recent N entries of demand history is used.

Table 3.2 First 12 months of moving average with parameter $N=10$

t	x(t)	N`	a`
11	10	1	10.00
2	12	2	11.00
3	6	3	9.33
4	9	4	9.25
5	4	5	8.20
6	10	6	8.50
7	6	7	8.14
8	7	8	8.00
9	9	9	8.11
10	8	10	8.10
11	13	10	8.40
12	11	10	8.30

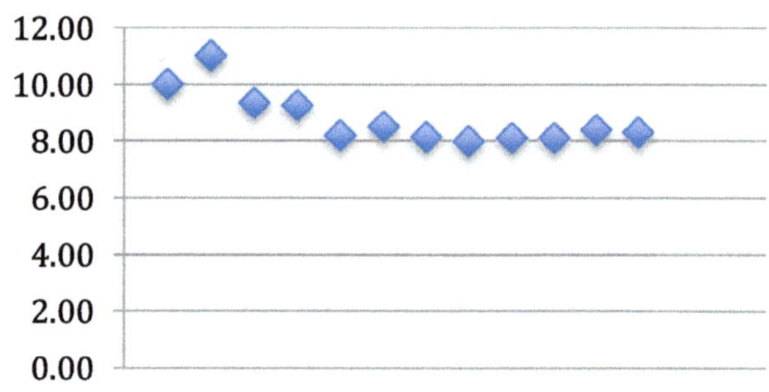

Fig. 3.2 Twelve months of the moving average for Example 3.2 with parameter $N=10$

The method is described using Example 3.2 at the point when nmh = 12 and $N=10$. The most recent 10 demand entries are: x(3), …, x(12), and the estimate of the level at that point is a` = 8.3. The residual errors for the $N=10$ demands are computed by e(t) = [x(t) − a`] for t = 3 to 12. The sum of square of residual errors is denoted as S(e) and the estimate of the standard deviation, s, is obtained as follows:

$$s = \sqrt{S(e)/(N-1)}$$

In the example, S(e) = 64.160b, $N=10$ and

$$\begin{aligned} s &= \sqrt{64.160/(10-1)} \\ &= \sqrt{7.118} \\ &= 2.67 \end{aligned}$$

Table 3.3 Twelve months of raw and integer forecasts for Example 3.2 when nmh = 12 and N = 10

τ	f(τ)	x`(τ)
1	8.3	8
2	8.3	9
3	8.3	8
4	8.3	8
5	8.3	9
6	8.3	8
7	8.3	8
8	8.3	8
9	8.3	9
10	8.3	8
11	8.3	8
12	8.3	9

The coefficient of variation becomes,

$$\text{cov} = s/a = 2.67/8.30 = 0.322$$

3.11 Horizontal Discount Forecasts

Discounting is used in forecasting when the forecaster wants to use a specified number of months history to generate the forecasts and also desires to apply higher weights to each more recent demand history in a relative manner. Two parameters are needed here: N = the number of months of history to use, and β (0 < β < 1) = the discount weight. The demand history is, x(1), …, x(N). The discount parameter, β, assigns the weight $w(t) = \beta^{(N-t)}$ to each demand history month t. The estimate of the level, a, is computed as shown below:

$$a` = \Sigma_{t=1}^{N} x(t)w(t) / \Sigma_{t=1}^{N} w(t)$$

In this way, the estimate of the level is a discount weighted average with relatively more weight assigned to each more recent month by a factor of β = 0.9.

Example 3.3 Suppose the forecaster wants to use the horizontal discount forecast model with N = 12 months of demand history and β = 0.9 as the discount parameter. Assume also the demand history is the same as listed in Example 3.1. Table 3.4 is a worksheet that lists the history months, t, the demand history, x(t), the discount weights by month, w(t), and the product, x(t)w(t), for t = 1 to 12. At the bottom of the table are the sums,

$$\Sigma_{t=1}^{12} w(t) = 7.176$$

$$\Sigma_{t=1}^{12} x(t)w(t) = 64.625$$

Table 3.4 Worksheet for Example 3.3 with history months, t, history demands, x(t), discount weights, w(t), and product, x(t)w(t)

t	x(t)	w(t)	x(t)w(t)
1	10	0.314	3.138
2	12	0.349	4.184
3	6	0.387	2.325
4	9	0.430	3.874
5	4	0.478	1.913
6	10	0.531	5.314
7	6	0.590	3.543
8	7	0.656	4.593
9	9	0.729	6.561
10	8	0.810	6.480
11	13	0.900	11.700
12	11	1.000	11.000
Sum		7.176	64.625

Using the above sums, the estimate of the level is obtained as follows:

$$\begin{aligned} a` &= \Sigma_{t=1}^{12} x(t)w(t)/\Sigma_{t=1}^{12} w(t) \\ &= 64.625/7.176 \\ &= 9.006 \end{aligned}$$

and thereby, the raw forecast for the 12 future months becomes,

$$f(\tau) = 9.006 \qquad \tau = 1 \text{ to } 12$$

Figure 3.3 depicts the 12 months of demand history and the corresponding 12 months of forecasts. Note the forecasts are the raw forecasts. In this example, the integer forecasts are set to $x`(\tau)=9$ for each of the future 12 months

3.12 Standard Deviation and Cov

The standard deviation of the forecast errors is estimated by using the weighted average of the residual errors from the past demand history. The method is described using the data of Example 3.3. The 12 demand entries are: x(1), …, x(12), and the estimate of the level is a` = 9.006b. The residual errors for the $N=12$ demands are

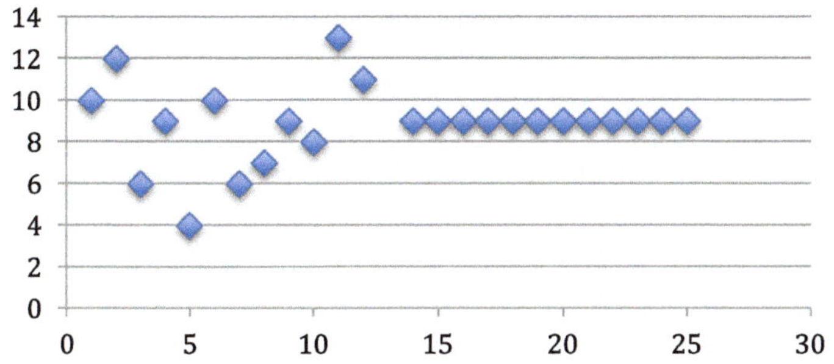

Fig. 3.3 Twelve months of demand history and 12 months of forecasts for Example 3.3 using the horizontal discount forecast model

computed by e(t) = [x(t) − a`] for t = 1 to 12. The discounted sum of square of residual errors is denoted as S(e) and is obtained as follows:

$$S(e) = \Sigma_{t=1}^{12}\left[w(t)e(t)^2\right]$$

So now, the estimate of the standard deviation of the forecast errors is computed as below:

$$s = \sqrt{S(e)/\Sigma_{t=1}^{12} w(t)}$$

Table 3.5 is a worksheet to compute the discount estimate of the standard deviation of the forecast error. The table lists the following: history months, t, demand history, x(t), forecast a`, residual error, e(t), the square of the residual error, the monthly discount weights, w(t), and the product, $w(t)e(t)^2$. At the bottom of the table are the sums:

$$\Sigma_{t=1}^{12} w(t) = 7.176$$

$$\Sigma_{t=1}^{12}\left[w(t)e(t)^2\right] = 46.576$$

Applying the discounted sums, the estimate of the standard deviation becomes,

$$\begin{aligned} s &= \sqrt{46.576/7.176} \\ &= \sqrt{6.491} \\ &= 2.55 \end{aligned}$$

Finally, the cov is,

$$cov = s/a\grave{} = 2.55/9.006 = 0.283$$

Table 3.5 Worksheet to compute the discount standard deviation of the forecast error, using history months, t, history demands, x(t), residual error, e(t), $e(t)^2$, the monthly discount weights, w(t), and product, $w(t)e(t)^2$

t	x(t)	a`	e(t)	$e(t)^2$	w(t)	$w(t)e(t)^2$
1	10	9.006	0.993	0.988	0.314	0.310
2	12	9.006	2.993	8.963	0.349	3.125
3	6	9.006	−3.006	9.037	0.387	3.501
4	9	9.006	−0.006	0.000	0.430	0.000
5	4	9.006	−5.006	25.061	0.478	11.987
6	10	9.006	0.993	0.988	0.531	0.525
7	6	9.006	−3.006	9.037	0.590	5.336
8	7	9.006	−2.006	4.024	0.656	2.640
9	9	9.006	−0.006	0.000	0.729	0.000
10	8	9.006	−1.006	1.012	0.810	0.820
11	13	9.006	3.993	15.951	0.900	14.356
12	11	9.006	1.993	3.976	1.000	3.976
Sum					7.176	46.576

3.13 Horizontal Smoothing Forecasts

The horizontal (exponentially) smoothing forecast model is used when the forecaster wants to revise the forecast each month with the most current demand entry, and also chooses to give higher weights to each more recent demand history in a relative manner. This method is often referred as exponential smoothing. One parameters is needed here, denoted as α ($0<\alpha<1$) where typically, $\alpha=0.10$.

To apply the model for a part at the current time, t, the data file houses the prior estimate of the level, a`(t−1), and retains the smooth parameter, α. Also, this is when the new demand entry becomes available, x(t). The two values, a`(t−1) and x(t) are now smoothed in the following way:

$$a`(t) = \alpha x(t) + (1-\alpha)a`(t-1)$$

The level becomes the estimate of the average value as of the most current month, t, and thereby the forecast for future month, τ, becomes,

$$f(\tau) = a`(t) \qquad \tau = 1, 2, \ldots..$$

A difficulty occurs at the outset when no history demands are available to use in smoothing. Further, in the early months, the forecaster may also wish to give higher weights to the demands. A way to overcome is the following. The forecaster specifies a parameter value to use, α, and for the early history months, the parameter is set as:

$$\alpha(t) = \max(\alpha, 1/t)$$

So now, the smoothed estimate of the level at month t is as follows:

$$a`(t) = \alpha(t)x(t) + [1 - \alpha(t)]a`(t-1)$$

3.14 Standard Deviation

The estimate of the standard deviation of the forecast error is also revised each month in the following way:

Let v(t) represent the estimate of the variance of the forecast error at time t. The data file on the part will save, a`(t−1), the estimate of the level, and v(t−1), the variance from the prior month (t−1). The forecast error at month t is now measured by

$$e(t) = x(t) - a`(t-1)$$

whereby, the revised variance becomes,

$$v(t) = \alpha(t)e(t)^2 + [1 - \alpha(t)]v(t-1)$$

So now, the estimate of the standard deviation of the forecast error at month t is:

$$s(t) = \sqrt{v(t)}$$

Finally, the associated cov becomes,

$$cov(t) = s(t)/a`(t)$$

Example 3.4 Consider an inventory system where the forecasts are generated using the horizontal smoothing model with the smoothing parameter set at $\alpha=0.10$. Assume at the first month of history, t=1, the demand entry is x(1)=22. Suppose also the forecaster uses the method described above to determine the smooth parameter for the early months. Hence,

$$\alpha(t) = \max(0.10, 1/t) \qquad t = 1, 2, \ldots$$

In the example, $\alpha(1)=1.00$, and the estimate of the level is

$$a`(1) = 1.00 \times 22 + (1-1) \times 0 = 22$$

Continuing at t=1, the forecasts for future month τ are,

$$f(\tau) = 22 \qquad \tau = 1, 2, \ldots$$

Note the prior estimate of the level is a`(0) = 0. Continuing are the computations (at t = 1) for the forecast error, variance, standard deviation and the coefficient of variation.

$$e(1) = [22 - 0] = 22$$

$$v(1) = 1.00 \times 22^2 + (1-1) \times 0 = 484$$

$$s(1) = \sqrt{482} = 22$$

and cov(1) = 22/22 = 1.00.

At t = 2, assume the demand is x(2) = 43. The corresponding computations are:

$$\alpha(2) = 1/2 = 0.50$$

$$a`(2) = 0.50 \times 43 + (1 - 0.5) \times 22 = 32.5$$

$$e(2) = 43 - 22 = 21$$

$$v(2) = 0.50 \times 21^2 + (1 - 0.50) \times 484 = 462.5$$

$$s(2) = \sqrt{462.5} = 21.5$$

and cov(2) = 21.5/32.5 = 0.662

Table 3.6 shows how the calculations would take place for the first 24 months of demands. The table lists the month, smooth parameter, demand, level, variance, standard deviation and the coefficient of variation for each month t. Since the specified smooth parameter is $\alpha = 0.10$, the smooth parameters are higher than 0.10 for the first 9 months. Thereafter, the desired smooth parameter (0.10) is used.

Note how the cov starts out as cov(1) = 1.00, and gradually decreases as the number of months of history increases. Near month t = 22, the cov settles in at about 0.30.

3.15 2-Stage Forecasts

In many inventory systems, the data saved for each part is the number of lines, n(t), and the demands, x(t), for each history month t. When each customer order comes into the order entry system, the order contains a finite number of lines, where each line is for an individual part. The line further states how many pieces, d, is needed for the part. So when a month has n(t) lines on a part, and the demand is x(t) for

Table 3.6 Horizontal smoothing forecasts for history months t=1 to 24, with smooth parameter, α(t), demand, x(t), level, a`(t), variance of forecast error, v(t), standard deviation of forecast error, s(t), and coefficient of variation, cov(t)

t	α(t)	x(t)	a`(t)	v(t)	s(t)	cov(t)
1	1.000	22	22.00	484.0	22.0	1.000
2	0.500	43	32.50	462.5	21.5	0.662
3	0.333	42	35.67	338.4	18.4	0.516
4	0.250	14	30.25	371.2	19.3	0.637
5	0.200	56	35.40	429.6	20.7	0.585
6	0.167	46	37.17	376.7	19.4	0.522
7	0.143	67	41.43	450.0	21.2	0.512
8	0.125	58	43.50	428.1	20.7	0.476
9	0.111	41	43.22	381.2	19.5	0.452
10	0.100	41	43.00	343.6	18.5	0.431
11	0.100	44	43.10	309.3	17.6	0.408
12	0.100	53	44.09	288.2	17.0	0.385
13	0.100	30	42.68	279.2	16.7	0.392
14	0.100	56	44.01	269.1	16.4	0.373
15	0.100	50	44.61	245.7	15.7	0.351
16	0.100	78	47.95	332.6	18.2	0.380
17	0.100	29	46.06	335.3	18.3	0.398
18	0.100	55	46.95	309.8	17.6	0.375
19	0.100	52	47.45	281.3	16.8	0.353
20	0.100	47	47.41	253.2	15.9	0.336
21	0.100	62	48.87	249.2	15.8	0.323
22	0.100	50	48.98	224.4	15.0	0.306
23	0.100	53	49.38	203.6	14.3	0.289
24	0.100	38	48.25	196.2	14.0	0.290

the month, $x(t)=d_{(1,t)}+\ldots+d_{(n(t),t)}$, where $d_{(i,t)}$ is the number of pieces for line i of month t. In most systems, the database will save the entries, n(t) and x(t), but not the individual line quantities, $d_{(i,t)}$.

3.16 Raw Lines to Integer Forecasts

When N months of data are saved, the following computations are as below:

$$\bar{n} = \sum_{t=1}^{N} n(t)/\mathrm{N} \quad = \text{average lines per month}$$

$$\mathrm{x(t)} = \sum_{i=1}^{n(t)} d_{(i,t)} \quad = \text{demands in month t}$$

Table 3.7 Example 3.5 data of lines per month, n(t), and demands per month, x(t)

t	n(t)	x(t)
1	1	3
2	0	0
3	2	5
4	1	2
5	0	0
6	3	4
7	2	3
8	1	4
9	0	0
10	0	0
11	1	3
12	2	4
Sum	13	28

$$\bar{d} = \sum_{t=1}^{N} x(t) \Big/ \sum_{t=1}^{N} n(t) = \text{average pieces per line}$$

$$\begin{aligned}\bar{x} &= \bar{n}\bar{d} \\ &= \sum_{t=1}^{N} x(t)/\text{N} \\ &= \text{average demand per month}\end{aligned}$$

The estimate of the level per month is:

$$\text{a}` = \bar{x}$$

and thereby, the raw forecast on the demand per month becomes:

$$\text{f(t)} = \text{a}` \quad \text{t} = 1, 2, \ldots$$

Note, the forecasts are based on raw forecast of the lines per month and also on the average pieces per line.

Example 3.5 Suppose a part where the demand history is as listed in Table 3.7. For each of the 12 months of history, the lines, n(t), and the demands, x(t), are saved. The sums for the two variables are at the bottom of the table where $\sum \text{n(t)} = 13$ and Sx(t)=28. Hence, the average lines per month becomes,

$$\bar{n} = 13/12 = 1.083$$

Table 3.8 Raw, f(τ), and integer, x`(τ), forecasts for 6 future months, τ, in Example 3.5

τ	f(τ)	x`(τ)
1	2.33	2
2	2.33	3
3	2.33	2
4	2.33	2
5	2.33	3
6	2.33	2

Table 3.9 Lines, n(t), and demands, x(t), per month for the part in Example 3.6

t	n(t)	x(t)
1	0	0
2	0	0
3	0	0
4	1	50
5	0	0
6	0	0
7	0	0
8	0	0
9	0	0
10	1	30
11	0	0
12	0	0
Sum	2	80

Also, the average pieces per line is

$$\bar{d} = 28/13 = 2.15$$

The estimate of the level is obtained from

$$a` = \sum x(t)/N{=}28/12 = 2.33$$

or from

$$a` = \bar{n}\bar{d} = 1.083 \times 2.15 = 2.33$$

Table 3.8 lists the forecasts for the first 6 future months. Note, the raw forecasts are f(τ) = 2.33, and the corresponding integer forecasts, x`(τ), become (2, 3, 2, 2, 3, 2).

Example 3.6 Consider another part where the lines and demands are saved in the data file, and these are listed in Table 3.9. This part has low demands where over the past 12 months, only two lines came in, one for 50 pieces and another for 30 pieces.

Table 3.10 Raw forecasts, f(τ), and integer forecasts, x`(τ), for the part in Example 3.6

t	f(τ)	x`(τ)
1	6.67	7
2	6.67	7
3	6.67	6
4	6.67	7
5	6.67	7
6	6.67	6
7	6.67	7
8	6.67	7
9	6.67	6
10	6.67	7
11	6.67	7
12	6.67	6

In this situation, the following averages are computed:

$$\bar{n} = 2/12 = 0.167 = \text{average lines per month}$$

$$\bar{d} = 80/2 = 40 = \text{average pieces per line}$$

The estimate of the level is $a` = \bar{d} \times \bar{n} = 40 \times 0.167 = 6.67$. Table 3.10 lists the raw and integer forecasts of this part for the future 12 months. Note, in this low line item, the forecasts don't look much like the history months.

3.17 Integer Lines to Integer Forecasts

Another way to generate the forecasts so they more closely resemble the flow of demands is shown in Table 3.11. In this situation, the raw and integer lines are forecast for each of the 12 future months. The raw lines are $\bar{n} = 0.17$ per month. The integer lines, n`(t), are zero's and one's, where months 3 and 10 have an integer forecast of one. The demands for these months becomes:

$$x`(t) = n`(t)\bar{d}$$

When n`(t) = 1, the forecast is 40, and when n`(t) = 0, the forecast is zero.

Table 3.11 Raw lines, $\overline{n}$, integer lines, n`(τ), and integer forecast of demands, x`(τ) for future months τ

τ	$\overline{n}$	n`(τ)	x`(τ)
1	0.17	0	0
2	0.17	0	0
3	0.17	1	40
4	0.17	0	0
5	0.17	0	0
6	0.17	0	0
7	0.17	0	0
8	0.17	0	0
9	0.17	0	0
10	0.17	1	40
11	0.17	0	0
12	0.17	0	0

Summary

Five horizontal forecast models are described. The horizontal forecast model is based on the N most prior monthly demands where each demand entry is assigned the same weight in generating the forecasts. The horizontal moving average forecast model uses a parameter N that specifies the number of most recent monthly demands to use in generating the forecasts. The method gives equal weight to each of the demands. A special adjustment is made for new parts when the number of history months is less than the parameter of N. The horizontal discounting forecast model is based on two parameters, N, the number of months of history to use, and β, the discount rate that assigns more weight to each more recent demand. The horizontal smoothing forecast model also gives more weight to the more recent demand entries. The model adjusts the prior forecast with the most current demand entry. The horizontal 2-stage forecast model generates a forecast for the number of lines by future months and then applies the average pieces-per-line to obtain the forecast of demands for each of the future months. This method may be useful when the history demands are of the lumpy type. For each of the forecast models, the methods generate raw forecasts that are in fractional form. A cumulative round algorithm converts the raw forecasts to integer forecasts. The standard deviation of the 1-month forecast error is also computed for the models. This is a measure on the accuracy of the forecasts and is needed in subsequent computations concerning the inventory replenishments in the stocking location. A relative way to measure the forecast error is by the coefficient of variation, denoted as cov.

Chapter 4
Trend Forecasts

4.1 Introduction

Some of the items stocked in the inventory have demand patterns where the month-to-month level is gradually increasing (or decreasing) in a steady way, and thereby, a trend forecast model is called. The model has two coefficients, a and b, where a is the intercept and b is the slope. Three such models are described here: trend regression forecasts, trend discount forecasts and trend smoothing forecasts. The trend regression forecast model generates a straight line fit through the most recent N history demands giving equal weight to each history demand. The trend discount forecast model also uses the N most recent history demands, but gives relatively less weight to each older demand. This model is based on a discount parameter, β, that specifies how to apportion the weight to each older demand entry. The trend smoothing forecast model revises the forecast coefficients as each new demand entry becomes available. The model has two parameters, α and β, that are used to revise the trend coefficients, (a, b), at each month. All three of the forecast models generate forecasts that are in fractional numbers and are here called raw forecasts. The forecasts are converted to integers using the cumulative rounding algorithm described in Chap. 2. For latter use, in inventory control, the standard deviation of each of the forecast models is also generated each month. For comparative sake, the coefficient of variation, cov, is also generated each month. Three dampening forecast models are described, to avoid situations when the forecasts are quickly declining to zero and below.

4.2 Trend Regression Forecast

The trend regression model generates a straight line fit through the past demands to project as forecasts for the future months. The model requires one parameter, N, that specifies the number of most recent past monthly demands to use in generating the forecasts. The history demands are labeled as, x(t) for t = 1 to N, and N is the most

N. T. Thomopoulos, *Demand Forecasting for Inventory Control*,
DOI 10.1007/978-3-319-11976-2_4

current history month, whereby t=1 is the oldest month. The forecast model has two coefficients, (a, b), where a is the intercept at t=0, and b is the slope. The fit of the demands over the N history months is denoted as f(t) where,

$$f(t) = a + bt \quad t = 1 \text{ to } N$$

The regression model is based on finding the estimates of the coefficients that minimize the sum of squares of residual errors, e(t), over the history months. The residual error for history month t is the following:

$$e(t) = [x(t) - f(t)]$$

The sum of square of the residual errors is denoted as S(e) where,

$$S(e) = \sum_{t=1}^{N} e(t)^2$$

A bit of calculus is used to determine how to find the fit that yields the least sum of squares of the residual errors. The minimum of S(e) requires finding the coefficients (a, b) that satisfy the following two equations:

$$\Sigma x = aN + b\Sigma t$$

$$\Sigma xt = a\Sigma t + b\Sigma t^2$$

where the sums are for t=1 to N. Also, for notational ease, $\Sigma t = \sum_{t=1}^{N} t$, $\Sigma t^2 = \sum_{t=1}^{N} t^2$, $\Sigma x = \sum_{t=1}^{N} x(t)$ and $\Sigma xt = \sum_{t=1}^{N} x(t)t$

Solving for the coefficients, yields,

$$b = [\Sigma x \Sigma t - N\Sigma xt] / [(\Sigma t)^2 - N\Sigma t^2]$$
$$a = [\Sigma x - b\Sigma t] / N$$

Recall, a is the intercept at t=0. In forecasting, the level is commonly used in its place and represents the average of the demands at t=N, the most current month. This also is the level at τ=0, where τ identifies the future months. For this purpose, the intercept, a, is converted to the level, a`, as follows:

$$a` = a + Nb$$

The forecast for future month τ becomes,

$$f(\tau) = a` + b\tau \qquad \tau = 1, 2, \ldots$$

Table 4.1 Demand history months, t, and history demands, x(t), for Example 4.1

t	x(t)
1	17
2	18
3	10
4	25
5	18
6	25
7	23
8	20
9	17
10	23
11	23
12	18

Example 4.1 Suppose a system where the trend regression forecast model is to be used on a part with $N = 12$ history months of demands, and the history demands are those listed in Table 4.1 as x(t).

Raw Forecasts To apply the model, the following computations and summations are carried out, and are listed below where the summations range from t = 1 to 12.

$$N = 12$$
$$\Sigma x = 237$$
$$\Sigma xt = 1596$$
$$\Sigma t = 78$$
$$\Sigma t^2 = 650$$

Solving for the coefficients (b, a) yields:

$$b = 0.388 \qquad = \text{slope}$$
$$a = 17.227 \qquad = \text{intercept at } t = 0$$

The level becomes,

$$a' = a + 12b = 21.885 \qquad = \text{level at } \tau = 0 \qquad (t = 12)$$

So now, the forecasts for each of the future 12 months are generated using:

$$f(\tau) = 21.885 + 0.388\tau \qquad \tau = 1 \text{ to } 12$$

Integer Forecasts Since the forecasts are in fractional form, the forecasts are raw forecasts. The corresponding integer forecasts, x`(τ), are also generated in the same

Table 4.2 Future months, τ, with raw forecasts, f(τ), and integer forecasts, x`(τ)

τ	f(τ)	x`(τ)
1	22.27	22
2	22.66	23
3	23.04	23
4	23.43	23
5	23.82	24
6	24.21	24
7	24.60	25
8	24.98	25
9	25.37	25
10	25.76	26
11	26.15	26
12	26.54	27

way as given in Chap. 2. Table 4.2 lists the raw and integer forecasts for the future 12 months. Figure 4.1 depicts the flow to the 12 months of history demands and the 12 months of integer forecasts.

Standard Deviation Table 4.3 is a worksheet to begin the calculations of estimating the standard deviation of the forecast errors. The table lists the 12 history months with the associated demand history. and the corresponding fit values, f(t). Next is a list of the residual errors, e(t) = [x(t) − f(t)], and then the square of e(t). The sum of the square of the residual errors is in the base of the table, and is denoted as S(e).

The estimate of the standard deviation, s, is as follows:

$$s = \sqrt{S(e)/(N-2)}$$

In the example,

$$s = \sqrt{184.71/(12-2)} = 4.30$$

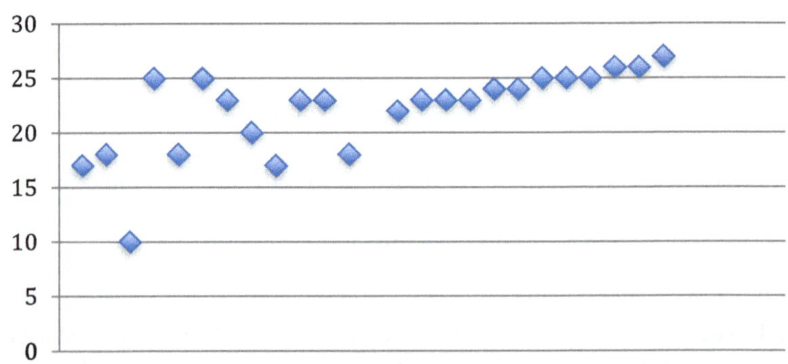

Fig. 4.1. Plot of 12 month history of demands and 12 future integer forecasts of Example 4.1

Table 4.3 Worksheet listing the history months, t, demand history, x(t), fit, f(t), residual errors, e(t), and square of residual errors, $e(t)^2$

t	x(t)	f(t)	e(t)	$e(t)^2$
1	17	17.61	−0.62	0.38
2	18	18.00	0.00	0.00
3	10	18.39	−8.39	70.42
4	25	18.77	6.22	38.69
5	18	19.16	−1.17	1.36
6	25	19.55	5.44	29.64
7	23	19.94	3.06	9.34
8	20	20.33	−0.33	0.11
9	17	20.72	−3.72	13.84
10	23	21.10	1.89	3.58
11	23	21.49	1.50	2.26
12	18	21.88	−3.88	15.09
Sum				184.71

Coefficient of Variation The coefficient of variation is measured using the level, a`, as the base. This is,

$$\text{cov} = s / a` = 4.30/21.885 = 0.196$$

4.3 Trend Discount Forecasts

The trend discount forecast model is the same as the trend regression forecast model except this model generates linear forecasts that give relatively more weight to each more recent history demand. The model requires two parameters, N and β. N states the number of history demands to use in generating the forecasts, and β is the discount parameter that specifies how much less weight to give to each older history demand. The history demands are labeled as, x(t) for t = 1 to N. The forecast model has two coefficients, (a, b), where a is the intercept at t = 0, and b is the slope. The fit of the demands over the N history months is denoted as f(t) where,

$$f(t) = a + bt \quad t = 1 \text{ to } N$$

The regression model is based on finding the estimates of the coefficients that minimize the weighted sum of squares of residual errors, e(t), over the history months. The residual error for history month t is the following:

$$e(t) = [x(t) - f(t)]$$

The discount parameter, β, falls in the interval $(0<\beta<1)$ The demand history is, x(1),…, x(N). The discount parameter, β, assigns the weight $w(t)=\beta^{(N-t)}$ to each history month t. In this way, the estimate of the forecast coefficients, (a, b), are obtained where a higher weight is assigned to each more recent month by a factor of β. A common value of the discount parameter used for the trend forecast model is $\beta=0.95$.

The weighted sum of square of the residual errors is denoted as S(e) and is computed by,

$$S(e)=\sum_{t=1}^{N} w(t)e(t)^2$$

A bit of calculus is used to determine how to find the fit that yields the least sum of squares of the weighted residual errors. The minimum of S(e) requires finding the coefficients (a, b) that satisfy the following two equations:

$$\begin{aligned}\Sigma\,\mathrm{xw} &= \mathrm{a}\Sigma\,\mathrm{w} + \mathrm{b}\Sigma\,\mathrm{tw}\\ \Sigma\,\mathrm{xtw} &= \mathrm{a}\Sigma\,\mathrm{tw} + \mathrm{b}\Sigma\,\mathrm{t}^2\mathrm{w}\end{aligned}$$

where the sums are for t=1 to N. Also, for notational ease, $\Sigma\,\mathrm{w} = \sum_{t=1}^{N} w(t)$, $\Sigma\,\mathrm{tw} = \sum_{t=1}^{N} tw(t)$, $\Sigma\,\mathrm{t}^2\mathrm{w} = \sum_{t=1}^{N} t^2 w(t)$, $\Sigma\,\mathrm{xw} = \sum_{t=1}^{N} x(t)w(t)$ and $\Sigma\,\mathrm{xtw} = \sum_{t=1}^{N} x(t)tw(t)$.

Solving for the coefficients, yields,

$$\begin{aligned}\mathrm{b} &= \left[\Sigma\,\mathrm{xw}\Sigma\,\mathrm{tw} - \Sigma\,\mathrm{w}\Sigma\,\mathrm{xtw}\right] \Big/ \left[(\Sigma\,\mathrm{tw})^2 - \Sigma\,\mathrm{w}\Sigma\,\mathrm{t}^2\mathrm{w}\right]\\ \mathrm{a} &= \left[\Sigma\,\mathrm{xw} - \mathrm{b}\Sigma\,\mathrm{tw}\right] / \Sigma\,\mathrm{w}\end{aligned}$$

As before, a is the intercept at t=0. In the notation here, the level represents the average value of the demands for the most current month, t=N. This also is the level at $\tau=0$, where τ represents the future months. Hence, the intercept, a, is converted to the level, a`, as follows:

$$\mathrm{a}` = \mathrm{a} + \mathrm{Nb}$$

So now, the forecast for future month τ becomes,

$$f(\tau) = \mathrm{a}` + \mathrm{b}\tau \qquad \tau = 1, 2, \ldots$$

Example 4.2 Suppose the forecaster now wants to apply the trend discount regression forecast model to the data of Example 4.1. The parameters are: $N=12$ for the number of history demand months, and $\beta=0.95$ for the discount weights. Table 4.4 is a list of the 12 months of demand history and the corresponding monthly discount weights. Note at t=12, $w(12)=0.95^{(12-12)}=1.000$; at t=11, $w(11)=0.95^{(12-11)}=0.95$, and so forth.

Table 4.4 Demand history months, t, demands, x(t), and discount weights, w(t), for Example 4.2

t	x(t)	w(t)
1	17	0.568
2	18	0.598
3	10	0.630
4	25	0.663
5	18	0.698
6	25	0.735
7	23	0.773
8	20	0.814
9	17	0.857
10	23	0.902
11	23	0.950
12	18	1.000

To apply the model, the following computations and summations are carried out, and are listed below.

$$\sum xw = 183.55$$
$$\sum xtw = 1339.59$$
$$\sum tw = 65.34$$
$$\sum t^2 w = 571.86$$
$$\sum w = 9.19$$

Raw Forecasts Solving for the coefficients (b, a) yields:

$$b = 0.326 \qquad = \text{slope}$$
$$a = 17.652 \qquad = \text{intercept at } t = 0$$

The level at t=N becomes,

$$a' = a + 12b = 21.561 \qquad = \text{level at } \tau = 0(t = 12)$$

So now, the forecasts for each of the future 12 months are generated using:

$$f(\tau) = 21.561 + 0.326\tau \qquad \tau = 1 \text{ to } 12$$

Integer Forecasts Since the forecasts are in fractional form, the forecasts are raw forecasts. The corresponding integer forecasts, x`(τ), are also generated in the same way as given in Chap. 2. Table 4.5 lists the raw and integer forecasts for the future 12 months. Figure 4.2 depicts the flow to the 12 months of history demands and the corresponding 12 months of integer forecasts.

Table 4.5 Future months, τ, raw forecasts, f(τ) and integer forecasts, x`(τ)

τ	f(τ)	x`(τ)
1	21.88	22
2	22.21	22
3	22.53	23
4	22.86	23
5	23.18	23
6	23.51	23
7	23.84	24
8	24.16	24
9	24.49	25
10	24.81	25
11	25.14	25
12	25.46	25

Table 4.6 is a worksheet to begin the calculations of estimating the standard deviation of the forecast errors. The table lists the 12 history months with the associated demand history, the discount weights, w(t), and the corresponding linear fit of the history months, f(t). Next is a list of the residual errors, e(t) = [x(t) − f(t)], and then the discount weighted square of e(t). The weighted sum of the square of the residual errors, S(e), is listed at the bottom of the table.

Standard Deviation The estimate of the standard deviation, s, is as follows:

$$s = \sqrt{S(e)/\Sigma w}$$

In the example,

$$s = \sqrt{132.23/9.19} = 3.793$$

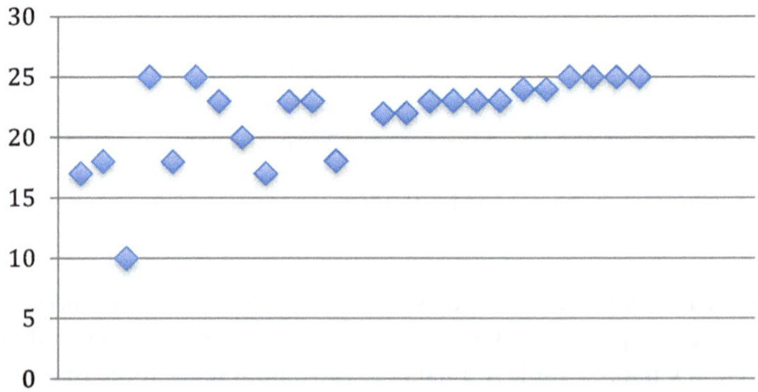

Fig. 4.2 Twelve months of demand history and 12 months of integer forecasts for Example 4.2

Table 4.6 Worsheet with history months, t, demand history, x(t), discount weights, w(t), fit of history months, f(t), residdual errors, e(t), and weighted square of residual errors, $e(t)^2w(t)$

t	x(t)	w(t)	f(t)	e(t)	$e(t)^2w(t)$
1	17	0.568	17.98	−0.98	0.54
2	18	0.598	18.30	−0.30	0.06
3	10	0.630	18.63	−8.63	46.93
4	25	0.663	18.95	6.05	24.24
5	18	0.698	19.28	−1.28	1.15
6	25	0.735	19.61	5.39	21.39
7	23	0.773	19.93	3.07	7.28
8	20	0.814	20.26	−0.26	0.05
9	17	0.857	20.58	−3.58	11.01
10	23	0.902	20.91	2.09	3.95
11	23	0.950	21.23	1.77	2.96
12	18	1.000	21.56	−3.56	12.68
Sum					132.23

Coefficient of Variation The coefficient of variation is measured using the level, a`, as the base. This is,

$$\begin{aligned} \text{cov} &= s / a` \\ &= 3.793 / 21.561 \\ &= 0.176 \end{aligned}$$

4.4 Trend Smoothing Forecasts

The trend (exponentially) smoothing forecast model is another popular way to forecast the demands that include a trend component. The forecast model at month t for future month τ is formulated as below:

$$f(\tau) = a(t) + b(t)\tau \quad \text{for } \tau = 1, 2, \ldots$$

The coefficients are the following:

a(t) = estimate of the level at month t
b(t) = estimate of the slope at month t

The model requires two parameters: α = smooth parameter for the level, and β = smooth parameter for the slope. The current month is labeled as t, and the estimates of the prior month's level and slope, are denoted as a(t-1) and b(t-1), respectively. At month t, the most current demand entry becomes available and is noted as x(t). As each month passes on, the estimates of the level and slope are revised in the following way:

$$a(t) = \alpha[x(t)] + (1-\alpha)[a(t-1) + b(t-1)]$$
$$b(t) = \beta[a(t) - a(t-1)] + (1-\beta)[b(t-1)]$$

Standard Deviation The estimate of the standard deviation of the one-month ahead forecast error is also revised at each month in the following way. The one-month ahead forecast error at month t is:

$$\begin{aligned} e(t) &= x(t) - f(t-1) \\ &= x(t) - [a(t-1) + b(t-1)] \end{aligned}$$

The estimate of the standard deviation of the one-month forecast error is smoothed and calculated as below:

$$s(t) = \sqrt{\alpha[e(t)^2] + (1-\alpha)[s(t-1)^2]}$$

where s(t− 1) is the standard deviation from the prior month, (t− 1), and s(t) is the standard deviation of the current month t.

Coefficient of Variation Finally, the coefficient of variation at month t is computed by,

$$cov(t) = s(t)/a(t)$$

Initial Forecast Adjustments When a part is new to the inventory system, there is no prior estimate of the level and slope, and thereby some minor adjustments to the computations are often applied.

An adjustment for this situation is described here. The smoothing parameter for the level, α, is adjusted each month in the following way:

$$\alpha(t) = \max(\alpha, 1/t) \quad t = 1,2,\ldots$$

This adjustment only pertains to the early months of a part's history. For example, if α = 0.20 is desired, the adjusted values of the parameter become: 1.00, 0.50, 0.33, 0.25, 0.20, 0.20,…for months, t = 1, 2, 3, 4, 5, 6, and remain at 0.20 for t = 5 or higher. This way, more weight is assigned to the early months, since there is minimum data, while the demands are (possibly) fluctuating more. So, for the early months, the smoothing parameter to estimate the level uses α(t) as described here.

Second, at the first month, t = 1, since there is no prior estimate of the level at t = 0, the estimate of the slope is automatically set to b(1) = 0. Hence, at t = 1, the estimates of the level and slope become,

$$a(1) = x(1)$$
$$b(1) = 0$$

Example 4.3 Suppose an inventory system is using the trend smoothing forecast model with parameters, $\alpha = \beta = 0.10$ where the parameter for the level is adjusted for the early months as described. A new part enters the system and the first month (t = 1) of demand becomes x(1) = 23 pieces. Note, the prior estimates of the coefficients are: a(0) = b(0) = 0.00.

At month t = 1, the following computations take place:

$$\alpha(1) = \max(0.10, 1/1) = 1.00$$
$$a(1) = 1.00x(1) + (1 - 1.00)[a(0) + b(0)] = x(1) = 23.00$$
$$b(1) = 0.00$$
$$f(\tau) = 23.00 + 0\tau \qquad \tau = 1, 2, \ldots$$
$$e(1) = x(1) - [a(0) + b(0)] = 23 - 0 = 23.00$$
$$s(1) = \{1.00 \times 23^2 + 0 \times 0\}^{0.5} = 23.00$$
$$cov(1) = s(1)/a(1) = 23.00/23.00 = 1.00$$

These measures are listed in Table 4.7 at t = 1.

Assume at month t = 2, the demand becomes, x(2) = 44. The smooth parameter for the level is now $\alpha(2) = 1/2 = 0.50$. Below are the calculations for this month:

$$a(2) = 0.50[44] + (1 - 0.50)[23.00 + 0.00] = 33.50$$
$$b(2) = 0.10[33.50 - 23.00] + (1 - 0.10)[0.00] = 1.05$$
$$f(t) = 33.50 + 1.05t \quad t = 1, 2, \ldots$$
$$e(2) = 44 - (23.00 + 0.00) = 21.00$$
$$s(2) = \{0.50 \times 21.00^2 + (1 - 0.50)23.00^2\}^{0.5} = 22.02$$
$$cov(2) = s(2)/a(2) = 22.02/33.50 = 0.657$$

The above measures are listed in Table 4.7 at t = 2.

Table 4.7 shows how the measures would appear as they progress from month to month for each of the first 24 months of the demand history. At each month, a new demand becomes available and the calculations are carried out, accordingly. Each month, the forecast model is revised, and for subsequent inventory needs, so also is the standard deviation of the one-month ahead forecast error. Note in the table where the coefficient of variation, cov, starts out high and as the months pass by, the cov gradually becomes lower, indicating, the forecasts are turning more reliable.

Figure 4.3 depicts how the estimates of the level has changed from the first month, t = 1, to the last month, t = 24, in the example. Figure 4.4 is a corresponding plot for the slope. Figure 4.5 is a plot that shows the relation with the demand history, x(t), and the one month ahead foread, f(t − 1), of the demand.

Table 4.7 Worksheet with month t, smooth parameter α(t), demand x(t), level a(t), slope b(t), forecast f(τ), forecast error e(t), square of forecast error $e(t)^2$, standard deviation s(t), and coefficient of variation cov(t)

t	α(t)	x(t)	a(t)	b(t)	f(τ)	e(t)	$e(t)^2$	s(t)	cov(t)
1	1.00	23	23.00	0.00	23.00	23.00	529.00	23.00	1.000
2	0.50	44	33.50	1.05	34.55	21.00	485.00	22.02	0.657
3	0.33	43	37.37	1.33	38.70	8.45	347.13	18.63	0.499
4	0.25	15	32.77	0.74	33.51	−23.70	400.75	20.02	0.611
5	0.20	57	38.21	1.21	39.42	23.49	430.93	20.76	0.543
6	0.17	47	40.68	1.34	42.02	7.58	368.69	19.20	0.472
7	0.14	69	45.87	1.72	47.59	26.98	420.02	20.49	0.447
8	0.13	60	49.14	1.88	51.02	12.41	386.76	19.67	0.400
9	0.11	44	50.24	1.80	52.04	−7.02	349.26	18.69	0.372
10	0.10	44	51.23	1.72	52.95	−8.04	320.80	17.91	0.350
11	0.10	47	52.36	1.66	54.01	−5.95	292.26	17.10	0.327
12	0.10	56	54.21	1.68	55.89	1.99	263.43	16.23	0.299
13	0.10	33	53.60	1.45	55.05	−22.89	289.48	17.01	0.317
14	0.10	59	55.45	1.49	56.93	3.95	262.09	16.19	0.292
15	0.10	53	56.54	1.45	57.99	−3.93	237.43	15.41	0.273
16	0.10	82	60.39	1.69	62.08	24.01	271.34	16.47	0.273
17	0.10	34	59.27	1.41	60.68	−28.08	323.05	17.97	0.303
18	0.10	59	60.51	1.39	61.90	−1.68	291.03	17.06	0.282
19	0.10	57	61.41	1.34	62.76	−4.90	264.33	16.26	0.265
20	0.10	52	61.68	1.23	62.92	−10.76	249.47	15.79	0.256
21	0.10	67	63.32	1.28	64.60	4.08	226.19	15.04	0.238
22	0.10	56	63.74	1.19	64.93	−8.60	210.96	14.52	0.228
23	0.10	58	64.24	1.12	65.36	−6.93	194.67	13.95	0.217
24	0.10	44	63.22	0.91	64.13	−21.36	220.81	14.86	0.235

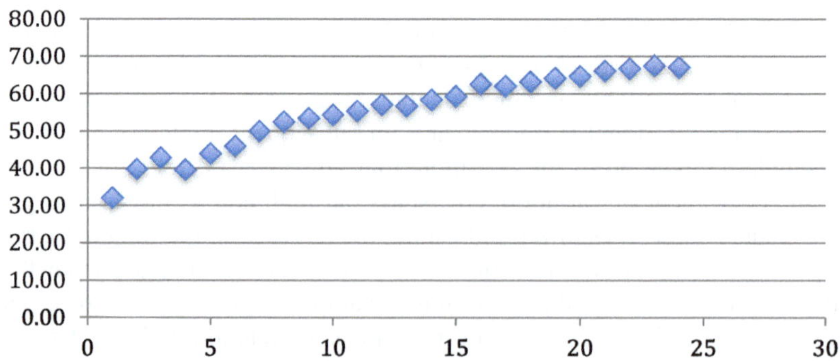

Fig. 4.3 Plot of the level coefficient, a(t), for t = 1 to 24

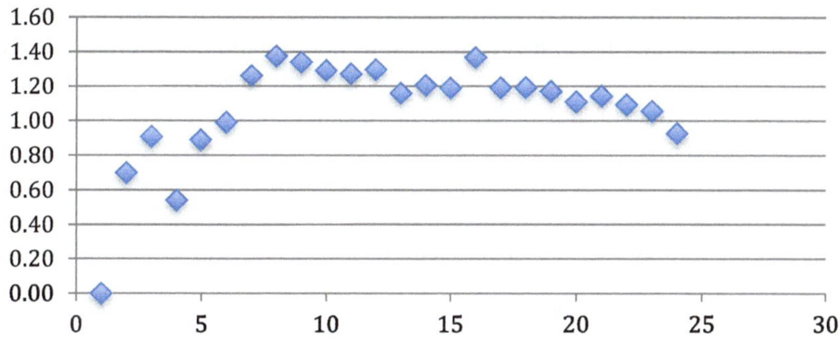

Fig. 4.4 Plot of the slope coefficient, b(t), for t=1 to 24

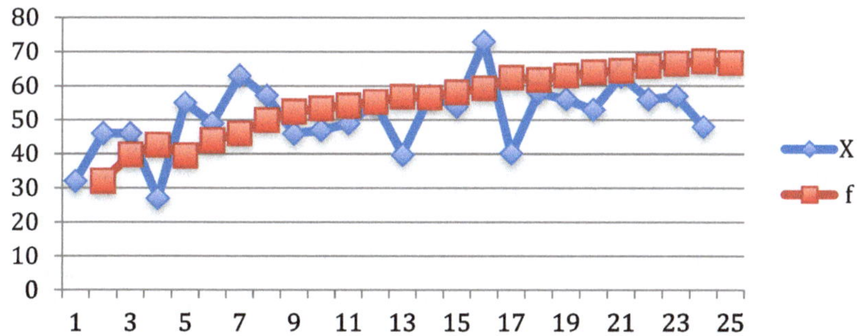

Fig. 4.5 Plot of the demands, x(t), and the 1 month ahead forecasts, f(t) for t=1 to 24

4.5 Dampening

Consider an item where a trend forecast model is being applied and the trend is declining and is swiftly approaching zero and below. Even though the trend is derived using the history of demands in a sound manner, the forecaster may wish to change the drop from a straight line leading to zero, to a flow that is always positive and is gradually approaching zero. The gradual flow to zero is in essence, how most items in the inventory die out anyway. This technique is called dampening and is an especially useful adjustment for fast declining forecasts. Three forecast models that use dampening are described is this section. These are the linear trend forecast model, the geometric forecast model and the maximum forecast model.

4.6 Linear Trend Forecast Model

Recall, the forecasts with a trend model have coefficients as listed below:

a = level as of the most current time period
b = slope

For convenience in this section, this is called a linear trend forecast model. When the forecast is declining, $b<0$, it is of interest to find the month where the forecasts will fall to zero. This is obtained by setting the forecast to zero ($x_L(\tau)=0$) and solving for τ. The particular month where the forecast reaches zero is denoted τ_o and is obtained as below:

$$\tau_o = -a/b$$

To avoid negative forecasts, the linear trend forecasts are adjusted as below:

$$x`_L(\tau) = \max(a + b\tau, 0) \quad \tau = 1, 2, \ldots$$

It is also useful to compute the all-time-forecast from the linear trend forecast model, denoted as $X`_L$. This is obtained using some algebra as below:

$$X`_L = \sum_1^{\tau o} x`_L(\tau) = -a(a+b)/(2b)$$

4.7 Geometric Forecast Model

Now consider another way to generate forecasts that are declining in a gradual manner. This is by way of the geometric forecast model, defined with two coefficients, a = level, and θ= growth rate. When θ lies between zero and one, the raw forecasts are dropping each month and never reach zero or below. The model is formulated as below:

$$x`_G(\tau) = a\theta^\tau \qquad \tau = 1, 2, \ldots$$

The all-time-forecast using the geometric model, denoted as $X`_G$, is obtained, using algebra, as below:

$$X`_G = \sum_1^{\infty} x`_G(\tau) = a\theta/(1-\theta)$$

It is also of interest to find the value of θ that allows the geometric forecast model to have the same all-time-forecast as the linear trend forecast model, whereby, $X`_G = X`_L$. This is by solving for the value of θ that equates the two all-time-forecasts, as shown below:

$$a\theta/(1-\theta) = -a(a+b)/(2b)$$

Using algebra, the particular value of θ is the following:

$$\theta = (a+b)/(a-b)$$

This is the value of θ to use when converting forecasts based on the linear trend model to forecasts using the geometric model. As stated earlier, the geometric forecasts will never fall to zero or below and the all-time-forecasts will be the same as the linear trend forecast model.

Table 4.8 Listing of the 12 future months, τ, the forecasts from the linear model, $x`_L(\tau)$, $\theta^\tau$, the forecasts from the geometric model, $x`_G(\tau)$, and from the maximum model, $x`_M(\tau)$

τ	$x_L`(\tau)$	θ^τ	$x_G`(\tau)$	$x`_M(\tau)$
1	9	0.818	8.182	9.000
2	8	0.669	6.694	8.000
3	7	0.548	5.477	7.000
4	6	0.448	4.481	6.000
5	5	0.367	3.666	5.000
6	4	0.300	3.000	4.000
7	3	0.245	2.454	3.000
8	2	0.201	2.008	2.008
9	1	0.164	1.643	1.643
10	0	0.134	1.344	1.344
11	0	0.110	1.100	1.100
12	0	0.090	0.900	0.900
	45		40.950	48.995

4.8 Maximum Forecast Model

A criticism of the geometric forecast model is that for the early months, the forecasts generated are smaller than the counterpart forecasts from the linear trend forecast model. Some forecasters are reluctant to accept this situation. A way to overcome is to select the maximum of the two forecasts, denoted as $x`_M(\tau)$, and this forecast is obtained as below:

$$x`_M(\tau) = \max\left(x`_L(\tau), x`_G(\tau)\right) \quad \tau = 1, 2, \ldots$$

Note for this formulation, the forecasts are declining each month, they never fall below zero, and the all-time-forecast is a bit larger than the counterpart all-time-forecasts of both the linear trend forecast model and the geometric forecast model.

Example 4.4 Suppose a situation where the trend model yields a level and trend of: ($a=10$ and $b=-1$), and the forecaster wants to explore the three models of forecasting for this situation.

Linear Trend Forecasts: The monthly forecasts using the linear trend model is listed as below:

$$x`_L(\tau) = \max\left[(10 - 1\tau), 0\right] \qquad t = 1, 2, \ldots$$

In Table 4.8, the first 12 future months, τ, are listed in column 1, and the linear trend forecasts, $x`_L(\tau)$, are in column 2. Note where the first month the demands reach zero is $\tau=10$, and this corresponds to:

$$\tau_o = -a/b = -10/-1 = 10$$

The all-time-forecast for the linear trend forecast model is computed as:

$$\begin{aligned} x`_L &= -a(a+b)/(2b) \\ &= -10(10-1)/(-2) \\ &= 45 \end{aligned}$$

This quantity agrees with the sum at the bottom of column 2 in the table.

Geometric Forecasts: A first step to apply the geometric forecast model is to determine the growth rate, θ, as shown below:

$$\begin{aligned} \theta &= (a+b)/(a-b) \\ &= (10-1)/(10+1) \\ &= 9/11 \end{aligned}$$

Hence, the forecasts are generated as below:

$$\begin{aligned} x`_L(\tau) &= a\theta^\tau \\ &= 10(9/11)^\tau \quad \tau = 1, 2, \ldots \end{aligned}$$

The values of θ^τ are listed in column 3 of the table, and the monthly geometric forecasts are in column 4.

The all-time-forecast using the geometric forecast model is computed as below:

$$\begin{aligned} X`_G &= a\theta/(1-\theta) \\ &= 10(9/11)/(1-9/11) \\ &= 45 \end{aligned}$$

Note, the sum of the forecasts for the first 12 months of the geometric model is listed at the bottom of column 4 and is 40.950, a bit smaller than the corresponding sum of 45 for the linear trend forecast.

Maximum Forecast: A third way to generate the forecasts for a fast declining item is the maximum forecast that is computed as below:

$$x`_M(\tau) = \max(x`_L(\tau), x`_G(\tau)) \quad \tau = 1, 2, \ldots$$

The results are listed in the fifth column of the table, $x`_M(\tau)$. Note the sum of the forecasts for the first 12 months is 48.995, which is higher than the counterpart sum from the linear trend forecast model.

Figure 4.6 is a plot of the 12 future forecasts using the linear trend forecast model, $x`_L(\tau)$, and the geometric trend forecast model, $x`_G(\tau)$. Figure 4.7 depicts the forecasts from the maximum forecast model, $x`_M(\tau)$.

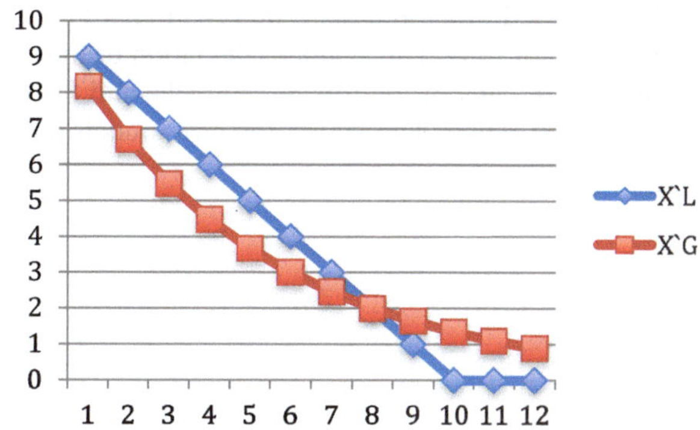

Fig. 4.6 Plot of the 12 months of forecasts from the linear forecast model, $x`_L(\tau)$, and from the geometric forecast model, $x`_G(\tau)$

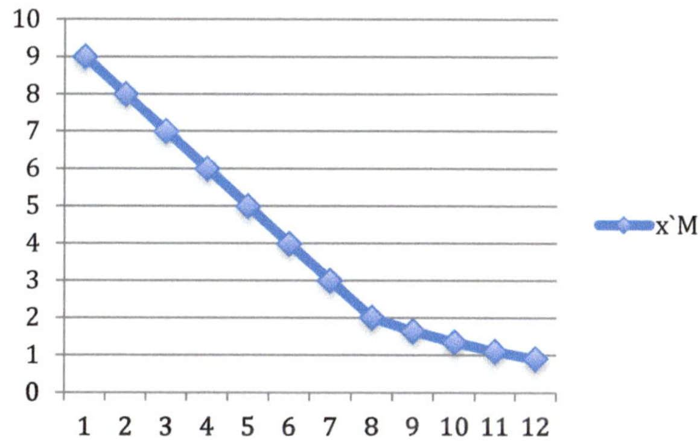

Fig. 4.7 Plot of the 12 months of forecasts from the maximum forecast model, $x`_M(\tau)$

4.9 Other Dampening Applications

Dampening can also be applied to the seasonal models of Chap. 5 and the promotion trend model of Chap. 6. The only portion of the seasonal and promotion models that are affected is the trend, $(a+b\tau)$.

Summary

Three forecast models are described that have a trend demand pattern, the trend regression forecast model, the trend discount forecast model and the trend smoothing forecast model. The trend regression model generates the forecasts using the most recent N monthly demands and assigns equal weight to each demand entry. The trend discount forecast model also uses the N most recent demand entries and gives relatively less weight to each older monthly demand entry. The trend smoothing forecast model revises the forecast each month with use of the most current demand entry. Each of the forecast models develops forecasts that are in numerical fractions and here called raw forecasts. The raw forecasts are converted to integer forecasts in a systematic way. The standard deviation of the one-month forecast error is also computed for each of the forecast models, and the coefficient of variation is computed as well. Three dampening forecast models are also described.

Chapter 5
Seasonal Forecasts

5.1 Introduction

Seasonal forecasts are needed when the demands over a year have a cyclical flow such as the rise for light clothing during the summers; heavy clothing during the winters, school supplies in late summers; antifreeze during the winters; golf balls in the summers; cold tablets in the winters; and sunglasses in the summers. Two forecast models are described: the seasonal smoothing multiplicative forecast model, and the seasonal smoothing additive forecast model. Perhaps the most common application of the model is when the demands are monthly covering 12 months in a year. The seasonal multiplicative model is described fully with example data. The model has two stages: first is to initialize the forecasts using the most current N history demands, and second is to revise the forecasts as each new monthly demand becomes available. The model includes a trend component and twelve seasonal ratios for each month of the year. The trend component could be flat, rising or falling, and the seasonal ratios could vary for each month of the year indicating an increase or decrease in the demands for the month relative to the trend. The model requires three smoothing parameters that assign higher weights to the more recent demands in the history. This way, the forecasts can readily react to any changes in the demand flow of the items in forecast. For brevity, an abridged discussion of the seasonal additive model is presented.

5.2 Seasonal Multiplicative Model

The seasonal (exponentially) smoothing multiplicative model applies when the demands follow a cyclical pattern from year to year, like the rise in the sale of bathing suits during the summer months. This demand flow is called a seasonal demand

N. T. Thomopoulos, *Demand Forecasting for Inventory Control*,
DOI 10.1007/978-3-319-11976-2_5

pattern and combines both seasonal and trend components. The forecast model for the τ-th future month, as of month t, is below:

$$f(\tau) = (a + b\tau)r(t+\tau) \quad \tau = 1, 2, \ldots$$

where: t is the current month, a is the level of the current month, b is the slope, and $r(t+\tau)$ is the seasonal ratio for the τ-th future month. The underlying trend of the seasonal pattern is measured by (a+bt). The seasonal ratios specify how the expected demand for the month will vary with respect to the trend. Altogether, there are 12 separate seasonal ratios, r(1),…, r(12), one for each month of the year and they repeat year after year. The seasonal ratios have an average of one and all are greater than zero. When $r(t)=1.00$, the expected demand for month t is the same as the trend; when $r(t)>1$, the expected demand for month t is larger than the trend; and when $r(t)<1$, the expected demand is below the trend.

The model is run in two stages: initialize and revise. The initialize stage is needed to estimate the 14 coefficients of the model (a, b, r(1),…, r(12)). The revise stage is used to update the model coefficients each month when a new demand entry becomes available.

Initialize Forecast Stage The initialize stage is described assuming 24 months of history demands are available. The demands are labeled as x(1),…, x(24) where x(1) is the oldest demand, and x(24) the most current.

The seasonal model also calls for three parameters, (α, β, γ), all in the range of zero to one, and typically, all are set near 0.10. The parameter α is used to smooth the estimate of the level, β to smooth the slope, and γ to smooth the seasonal ratios.

Below is an overview of the ten steps in the initialize stage.

1. X1 is the average of the first 12 history demands.
2. X2 is the average of the last 12 history demands.
3. b`(0) is the estimate of the slope at t=0.
4. a`(0) is the estimate of the level at t=0.
5. a`(t) is the estimate of the level at month t for t=1 to 24.
6. r`(t) is a measure of the seasonal ratio at t=1 to 24.
7. r(t) is an average estimate of the seasonal ratio at t=1 to 12.
8. Let a(0)=a`(0) and b(0)=b`(0).
9. Smoothed estimates of a(t), b(t) and r(t) are derived one month at a time starting with month t=1 and continuing till t=24.
10. At t=24, the initial forecast for future month τ is: $f(\tau)=[a(24)+b(24)\tau]r(24+\tau)$.

In a more detailed mathematical way, the ten steps to initialize the seasonal model listed above are below:

1. X1 = [x(1) + ... + x(12)]/12
2. X2 = [x(13) + ... + x(24)]/12
3. b\`(0) = [X2 – X1]/12
4. a\`(0) = X1 – 6.5b\`(0)
5. a\`(t) = a\`(0) + b\`(0)t   t = 1 to 24
6. r\`(t) = x(t)/a\`(t)   t = 1 to 24
7. r(t) = [r\`(t) + r\`(t+12)]/2   t = 1 to 12
8. a(0) = a\`(0) and b(0) = b\`(0)
9. Do the following for t = 1 to 24
   a(t) = α [x(t)/r(t)] + (1-α)[a(t-1)+b(t-1)]
   b(t) = β [a(t) – a(t-1)] + (1-β)[b(t-1)]
   r(t+12) = γ [x(t)/a(t)] + (1-γ)[r(t)]

Because t=24 is the final history month, the forecasts for the τ-th future month, as of t=24, is computed as below:

$$f(\tau) = [a(24) + b(24)\tau]r(24+\tau) \quad \tau = 1, 2, \ldots$$

It is important to synchronize the 12 unique seasonal ratios to the months following the most current month, t=24. For example, if month t=24 is March, then arrange for the seasonal ratio of the subsequent months to begin with April, and so forth.

Example 5.1 Suppose a system where the 24 months of demand history are those listed in Table 5.1 in the column, x(t). In the example, the smoothing parameters are (α=0.10, β=0.10 and γ=0.10). The following is a summary of the nine initialize steps.

1. X1 = [12 + ... + 11]/12 = 20.91
2. X2 = [13 + ... + 26]/12 = 27.33
3. b(0) = (27.33 – 20.91)/12 = 0.534
4. a(0) = 20.91 – 6.5×0.534 = 17.441
5. a(t) = 17.441 + 0.534t   t = 1 to 24 (column 3)
6. r\`(t) is computed for t = 1 to 24, (column 4)
7. r(t) is the average of months t and t+12 for t = 1 to 12, (column 5)
8. a(0) = 17.441 and b(0) = 0.534
9. The smoothing for t = 1 to 24 is as below:
   a(t) = 0.1 [x(t)/r(t)] + 0.9[a(t-1)+b(t-1)]   (column 6)
   b(t) = 0.1 [a(t) – a(t-1)] + 0.9b(t-1)]   (column 7)
   r(t+12) = 0.1[x(t)/a(t)] + 0.9[r(t)]   (column 8)

Table 5.1 Initialize worksheet for seasonal smoothing model, with history month t, demand history x(t), level a′(t), seasonal ratio r′(t), seasonal ratio r(t), level a(t), slope b(t), seasonal ratio r(t+12), fit f(t), and residual error e(t)

t	x(t)	a′(t)	r′(t)	r(t)	a(t)	b(t)	r(t+12)	f(t)	e(t)
1	12	17.73	0.68	0.61	17.93	0.55	0.61	11.01	0.99
2	22	18.26	1.20	0.72	19.67	0.67	0.76	15.02	6.98
3	27	18.80	1.44	1.31	20.37	0.68	1.31	26.77	0.23
4	22	19.33	1.14	1.11	20.92	0.66	1.11	23.15	−1.15
5	19	19.86	0.96	1.41	20.77	0.58	1.36	28.27	−9.27
6	27	20.40	1.32	1.65	20.85	0.53	1.61	33.67	−6.67
7	44	20.93	2.10	1.67	21.88	0.58	1.71	37.33	6.67
8	21	21.47	0.98	1.01	22.29	0.57	1.00	22.35	−1.35
9	15	22.00	0.68	0.82	22.41	0.52	0.80	17.96	−2.96
10	21	22.54	0.93	0.91	22.93	0.52	0.91	20.98	0.02
11	7	23.07	0.30	0.37	22.99	0.47	0.37	8.40	−1.40
12	11	23.61	0.47	0.52	23.25	0.45	0.51	11.90	−0.90
13	13	24.14	0.54		23.47	0.43	0.60	14.14	−1.14
14	6	24.68	0.24		22.34	0.27	0.68	15.16	−9.16
15	30	25.21	1.19		22.64	0.28	1.31	29.75	0.25
16	28	25.75	1.09		23.14	0.30	1.12	25.97	2.03
17	49	26.28	1.86		24.57	0.41	1.47	36.08	12.92
18	53	26.82	1.98		25.69	0.48	1.69	43.45	9.55
19	34	27.35	1.24		25.59	0.42	1.64	41.92	−7.92
20	29	27.89	1.04		26.29	0.45	1.02	26.77	2.23
21	27	28.42	0.95		27.37	0.52	0.83	22.80	4.20
22	26	28.95	0.90		27.94	0.52	0.92	25.61	0.39
23	13	29.49	0.44		29.11	0.59	0.38	11.05	1.95
24	17	30.02	0.57		30.02	0.62	0.52	15.64	1.36

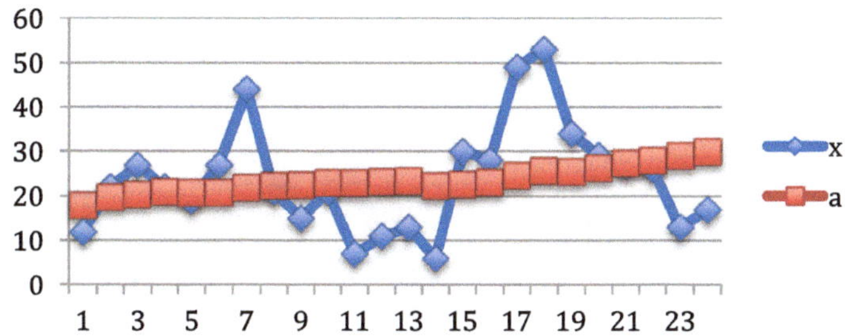

Fig. 5.1 Plot of 24 months of demand history, x(t), and the corresponding, level, a(t)

Initial Forecasts The initialize stage is now complete, and the initial forecast as of month t=24 for the τ-th future month is the following:

$$f(\tau) = [a(24) + b(24)\tau]r(24+\tau) \quad \tau = 1, 2, \ldots$$
$$= [30.02 + 0.62\tau]r(24+\tau)$$

Note, the seasonal ratios, at t=24, for the future months are listed in column 8 under r(t+12). So for the first future month, the seasonal ratio is for month t=(24+1)=25, and this is found in the row when t=13 and the seasonal ratio is r(13+12)=0.60. In a like way, all of the seasonal ratios for the future months are obtained. The forecasts for the first three future months are listed below:

τ	f(τ)
1	$[30.02 + 0.62 \times 1]0.60 = 18.38$
2	$[30.02 + 0.62 \times 2]0.68 = 21.26$
3	$[30.02 + 0.62 \times 3]1.31 = 41.76$

Seasonally Adjusted Average Figure 5.1 depicts the flow of the demand history, x(t), and the estimates of the associated level, a(t), for each of the months t=1 to 24. Recall, the level estimates the *seasonally adjusted average* for the month. The figure shows where the level is slightly increasing each month.

Fitted Values The fitted values are also listed in Table 5.1 for each of the history months, t=1 to 24. The fit is denoted as f(t) and is computed by, f(t)=a(t)×r(t). For example, at t=10, a(10)=23.935 and r(10)=0.915, thereby, f(10)=23.935×0.915=20.986. For brevity, the table only lists two decimals in the columns, while the computations are based on the higher fractional values. Figure 5.2 is a plot showing the relationship between the demand history, x(t), and the associated fitted value, f(t), for each month in the history.

Residual Errors The residual errors, e(t), are also listed in Table 5.1 for each of the history months, t=1 to 24. These are computed by

$$e(t) = x(t) - f(t).$$

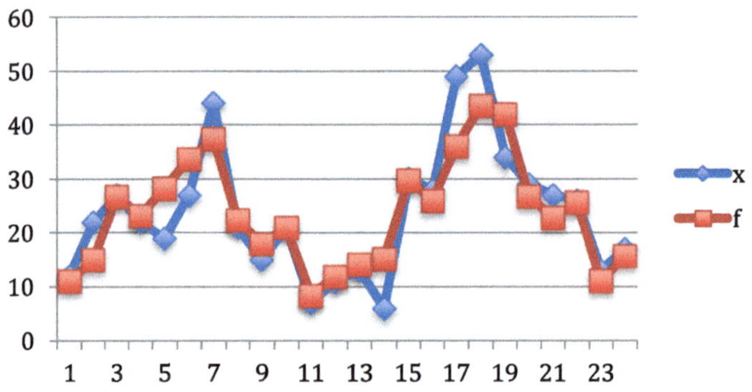

Fig. 5.2 Plot of 24 months of demand history, x(t), and the corresponding fit, f(t)

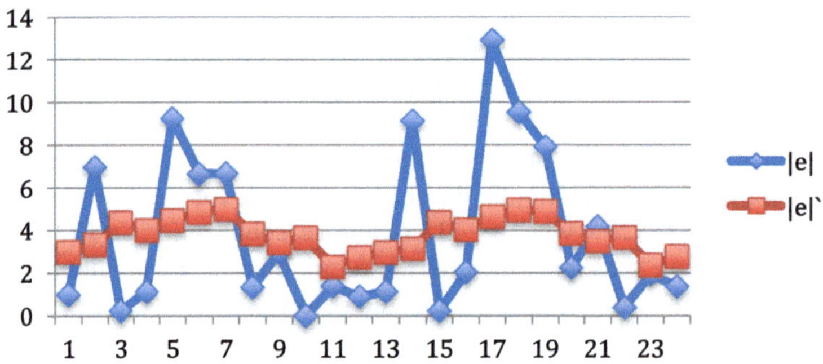

Fig. 5.3 Plot of absolute residual error, $|e|$, and fit $|e|^{`}$ over 24 months of history

At month t = 10, say, x(10) = 21, f(10) = 20.98, and thereby e(10) = (21 − 20.98) = 0.02.

In general, the absolute values of the residual errors will tend to flow higher and lower in a direct relation with the seasonal ratios. The lower the seasonal ratio for a month, the smaller the absolute values tend to be, and so forth. In Table 5.1, the average of the monthly absolute value is $|\bar{e}| = 3.83$. Figure 5.3 depicts the flow of the absolute values, |e| for each of the history months. The table also lists a pseudo way to generate a fitted value of the absolute value, denoted as $|e|^{`}$. The fitted values are computed in the following way:

$$|e(t)|^{`} = 3.83 \times \sqrt{r(t)} \text{ for } t = 1 \text{ to } 24$$

Note at t = 10, r(10) = 0.91, and thereby,

$$|e(10)|^{`} = 3.83 \times \sqrt{0.91} = 3.63$$

Figure 5.3 depicts the flow of the fitted error values for each of the 24 history months. The flow shows where the absolute values of the residual errors appear to rise and fall in the same direction as the fitted values. The swing is also in the same direction as the seasonal ratios.

Standard Deviation An estimate of the standard deviation of the forecast errors is computed as shown below where $s(t)^2$ is the standard deviation squared at month t.

$$\text{At } t = 1: s(1)^2 = e(1)^2$$

$$\text{For } t = 2 \text{ to } N: s(t)^2 = \alpha e(t)^2 + (1-\alpha)s(t)^2$$

The estimate of the standard deviation for the item is the final one, $s(t)^2$, computed at t=N, i.e.,

$$s = \sqrt{s(N)^2}$$

In the example,

$$s = 5.55$$

Assuming the pseudo fitted relation sited above with the absolute residual errors, the following rule-of-thumb may be applied with respect to the estimate of the standard deviation of the forecast error for each month. This is the following:

$$\begin{aligned} s(r) &= s\sqrt{r} \\ &= 5.55\sqrt{r} \end{aligned}$$

where s(r) is the standard deviation for a month, t, with the seasonal ratio set as r=r(t).

For example, s=5.55, and at month t=10, r(10)=0.91, thereby,

$$\begin{aligned} s(0.91) &= 5.55\sqrt{0.91} \\ &= 5.29 \end{aligned}$$

5.3 Revised Forecasts

After completing the initial stage, the forecasts are revised each month when a new demand entry becomes available. The revision uses smoothing, with the same parameters, (α, β, γ), as in the initialize stage. As each month t passes on, and a new demand entry, x(t), becomes available, the three model coefficients are revised as below:

$$a(t) = \alpha[x(t)/r(t)] + (1-\alpha)[a(t-1) + b(t-1)]$$

$$b(t) = \beta[a(t) - a(t-1)] + (1-\beta)[b(t-1)]$$

$$r(t+12) = \gamma[x(t)/a(t)] + (1-\gamma)[r(t)]$$

And as before, the forecast at month t for future month τ is the following:

$$f(\tau) = [a(t) + b(t)\tau]r(t+\tau) \quad t = 1, 2, \ldots$$

Example 5.2 Continuing with Example 5.1, suppose the demand at month t=25 is x(25)=15. So now the revised coefficients are computed as below:

$$a(25) = 0.1\times 15 + 0.9\times[30.02 + 0.62] = 29.076$$

$$b(25) = 0.1\times[29.076 - 30.02] + 0.9\times 0.62 = 0.464$$

$$r(36) = 0.1\times[15/29.076] + 0.9\times 0.60 = 0.5916$$

The τ month ahead forecasts as of month t=25 becomes,

$$f(\tau) = [29.076 + 0.464\tau]r(25+\tau) \quad \tau = 1, 2, \ldots$$

At τ=1,

$$\begin{aligned} f(1) &= [29.076 + 0.464\times 1]r(26) \\ &= [29.076 + 0.464]0.68 \\ &= 20.09 \end{aligned}$$

and so forth.

5.4 Initialize with 12-Months of Demand History

When 12 months of demand history are available, [x(1),…, x(12)], the seasonal multiplicative model can be initialized as described below:

$$X1 = [x(1) + \ldots + x(12)]/12 = \text{average demand for year 1}$$

$$a`(12) = X1 = \text{estimate of level at month } t = 12$$

$$b`(12) = 0.0 = \text{estimate of slope at month } t = 12$$

$$r(t+12) = x(t)/X1 \quad \text{for } t = 1 \text{ to } 12 = \text{estimate of seasonal ratios for 12 months}$$

5.5 Seasonal Additive Model

The additive version of the seasonal smoothing model is almost the same as the multiplicative version. Instead of using seasonal ratios as the multiplicative model does, the additive model uses seasonal increments that can be plus or minus. The initializing steps and the revision steps are almost the same in both models. For brevity, the description below is given without an example to illustrate the steps.

Initialize Forecast Stage The initialize stage is described assuming 24 months of history demands are available. The demands are labeled as x(1),…, x(24) where x(1) is the oldest demand, and x(24) the most current.

The seasonal model also calls for three parameters, (α, β, γ), all in the range of zero to one, and typically, all are set near 0.10. The parameter α is used to smooth the estimate of the level, β to smooth the slope, and γ to smooth the seasonal increments.

Below is an overview of the ten steps in the initialize stage.

1. X1 is the average of the first 12 history demands.
2. X2 is the average of the last 12 history demands.
3. b`(0) is the estimate of the slope at t=0.
4. a`(0) is the estimate of the level at t=0.
5. a`(t) is the estimate of the level at month t for t=1 to 24.
6. d`(t) is a measure of the seasonal increment at t=1 to 24.
7. d(t) is an average estimate of the seasonal increment at t=1 to 12.
8. Let a(0)=a`(0) and b(0)=b`(0).
9. Smoothed estimates of a(t), b(t) and d(t) are derived one month at a time starting with month t=1 and continuing till t=24.
10. At t=24, the initial forecast for future month τ is:
    $f(\tau)=[a(24)+b(24)\tau+d(24+\tau)]$

In a more detailed mathematical way, the ten steps to initialize the seasonal additive model listed above are below:

1. X1 = [x(1) + … + x(12)]/12
2. X2 = [x(13) + … + x(24)]/12
3. b`(0) = [X2 – X1]/12
4. a`(0) = X1 – 6.5b`(0)
5. a`(t) = a`(0) + b`(0)t   t = 1 to 24
6. d`(t) = [x(t) - a`(t)]   t = 1 to 24
7. d(t) = [d`(t) + d`(t+12)]/2   t = 1 to 12
8. a(0) = a`(0) and b(0) = b`(0)
9. Do the following for t = 1 to 24
    $a(t) = \alpha\,[x(t) - d(t)] + (1-\alpha)[a(t-1)+b(t-1)]$
    $b(t) = \beta\,[a(t) - a(t-1)] + (1-\beta)[b(t-1)]$
    $d(t+12) = \gamma\,[x(t) - a(t)] + (1-\gamma)[d(t)]$

Because t=24 is the final history month, the forecasts for the τ-th future month, as of t=24, is computed as below:

$$f(\tau) = [a(24) + b(24)\tau + d(24+\tau)] \quad \tau = 1, 2, \ldots$$

It is important to synchronize the 12 unique seasonal increments to the months following the most current month, t=24. For example, if month t=24 is March, then arrange for the seasonal increments of the subsequent months to begin with April, and so forth.

5.6 Initialize With 12-Months of Demand History

When 12 months of demand history are available, [x(1),..., x(12)], the seasonal additive model can be initialized as described below:

$$X1 = [x(1) + \ldots + x(12)]/12 = \text{ average demand for year 1}$$

$$a`(12) = X1 = \text{estimate of level at month } t = 12$$

$$b`(12) = 0.0 = \text{estimate of slope at month } t = 12$$

$$d(t+12) = [x(t) - X1] \quad \text{for } t = 1 \text{ to } 12$$
$$= \text{ estimate of seasonal additives for 12 months}$$

5.7 Revision Forecasts

After the initialize stage passes, the forecasts coefficients are revised each month with the arrival of a new demand entry, x(t). The revision steps for the three forecast coefficients are listed below:

$$a(t) = \alpha[x(t) - d(t)] + (1-\alpha)[a(t-1) + b(t-1)]$$

$$b(t) = \beta[a(t) - a(t-1)] + (1-\beta)[b(t-1)]$$

$$d(t+12) = \gamma[x(t) - a(t)] + (1-\gamma)[d(t)]$$

Upon the revision, the new forecast as of time t for the τ-th future month becomes the following:

$$f(\tau) = [a(t) + b(t)\tau + d(t+\tau)] \quad \tau = 1, 2, \ldots$$

Summary

The seasonal multiplicative model has components for the trend and monthly seasonal ratios. The model is run with two stages, the initial stage and the revision stage. This chapter shows how the initial stage estimates the fourteen model coefficients using the most recent months of demand history. Three parameters are used in the process, one to smooth the level, another to smooth the slope, and a third to smooth the seasonal ratios. Upon completing the initial stage, the initial forecasts can be generated. The chapter also shows how to compute an estimate of the standard deviation of the 1-month forecast error. Subsequent to the initial stage, the revision stage is run after each new monthly demand entry becomes available. With each new month, when a new demand entry becomes available, the model coefficients are revised by smoothing, and refreshed forecasts are generated. A brief review of the seasonal additive model is also presented.

Chapter 6
Promotion Forecasts

6.1 Introduction

Promotions come in various ways: price reduction, buy one get one free, zero interest, no money down, and so on. They often occur when a supplier or a stock location offers a price incentive of some sort to the customers to buy now with enticements for purchases more often or in larger quantities. The promotion typically has a start-date and end-date, and the demand during these days is relatively higher than the normal non-promo days. This situation causes wild fluctuations in the demand history and upsets the forecasting model in use. The standard deviation increases and the forecast coefficients swing out of normal control. Special adjustments are needed in the forecast models to overcome the fluctuations. Two forecast models are described here to accommodate the promotion activity: the promotion horizontal model and the promotion trend model. Both of the models involve two stages: the initial stage and the revision stage. The initial stage is the first estimates of the coefficients of the model. This stage requires N history months of demands and promotion measures. The coefficients of the model are estimated using regression methods where equal weight is given to each of the history months. The revision stage is used for the months after the initial stage where the coefficients are revised every month with each current month's data using the smoothing method. Estimates of the standard deviation and the coefficient of variation are computed for each of the two stages.

6.2 Promotion Horizontal Model

The promotion horizontal model is based on the most recent N months of demand and promotion history. The demands are denoted as x(t) and the promotions are p(t) for t = 1 to N, where t = 1 is the oldest month and t = N is the most current month. The model is of the following form:

N. T. Thomopoulos, *Demand Forecasting for Inventory Control*,
DOI 10.1007/978-3-319-11976-2_6

$$f(t) = a + cp(t)$$

where f(t) is the fitted value at history month t, and p(t) is the corresponding promotion measure at t. The promotion, p(t), could be a measure of the portion of month t that is active with a promotion. The two coefficients are (a, c), where a, is the estimate of the level, and c is the promo coefficient.

To apply, the model requires two stages, initialize and revision as described below. The initialize stage uses regression to estimate the coefficients of the model, and the revision stage uses smoothing.

6.3 Initialize Stage

The initialize first stage requires some history data for the part. The data comes from the most recent N months of demand and promotion history. The history months are t=1,…., N. The demand history is x(1),…, x(N), and the promotion history is p(1),…, p(N). Regression analysis is used to estimate the coefficients for the level and promotion coefficients.

Using the least squares method in the typical way, the following two equations are generated to obtain the two unknown coefficients, (a, c).

$$\sum x = (N)a + \left(\sum p\right)c$$
$$\sum xp = \left(\sum p\right)a + \left(\sum p^2\right)c$$

For notational ease, the following summation substitutions are used:

$$\sum_{t=1}^{N} x(t) = \sum x$$
$$\sum_{t=1}^{N} p(t) = \sum p$$
$$\sum_{t=1}^{N} x(t)p(t) = \sum xp$$
$$\sum_{t=1}^{N} p(t)^2 = \sum p^2$$

Below shows how to compute the coefficients.

$$c` = \left[\Sigma x \Sigma p - \Sigma xpN\right] / \left[(\Sigma p)^2 - \Sigma p^2 N\right]$$
$$a` = \left[\Sigma x - c`\Sigma p\right] / N$$

Table 6.1 Example 6.1 data: history month t, demand history x(t), and promotion p(t)

t	x(t)	p(t)
1	9	0
2	13	0
3	38	0.4
4	18	0.2
5	6	0
6	7	0
7	13	0
8	26	0.5
9	6	0
10	10	0
11	4	0
12	8	0

The fitted values over the history months are calculated as follows:

$$f(t) = a\grave{}+c\grave{}p(t) \quad t = 1 \text{ to } N$$

For each of the history months, the residual errors, e(t), are obtained in the following way:

$$e(t) = x(t) - f(t)$$

The residual errors are used to estimate the standard deviation of the one month forecast error, denoted as s. To apply, the sum of the square of the residual errors is tallied, $\Sigma e(t)^2$, and is used as follows:

$$s = \sqrt{\Sigma e(t)^2/(N-2)}$$

Finally, the coefficient of variation, cov, for the forecast error is computed using the estimate of the standard deviation, s, and the level, a`, as follows:

$$\text{cov} = s/a\grave{}$$

Example 6.1 Suppose the forecaster wishes to apply the promotion horizontal regression model for an item with N = 12 months of past history of demands and promotion as listed in Table 6.1.

Table 6.2 Worksheet for history months t, with demand history x(t), promotion p(t), fit f(t), and residual error e(t)

t	x(t)	p(t)	f(t)	e(t)
1	9	0	8.62	0.38
2	13	0	8.62	4.38
3	38	0.4	28.46	9.54
4	18	0.2	18.54	−0.54
5	6	0	8.62	−2.62
6	7	0	8.62	−1.62
7	13	0	8.62	4.38
8	26	0.5	33.42	−7.42
9	6	0	8.62	−2.62
10	10	0	8.62	1.38
11	4	0	8.62	−4.62
12	8	0	8.62	−0.62

The summations described above are the following:

$$\sum x = 158$$
$$\sum p = 1.1$$
$$\sum xp = 31.8$$
$$\sum p^2 = 0.45$$

The coefficient estimates are listed below:

$$a` = 8.621$$
$$c` = 49.59$$

and thereby, the fitted values for the history months are obtained by the relation,

$$f(t) = 8.621 + 49.59p(t) \quad t = 1 \text{ to } 12$$

Table 6.2 lists the fitted values, f(t), and the corresponding residual errors, e(t), for the history months. The residual error for month t is obtained by: e(t)=x(t)—f(t). Figure 6.1 depicts the relation between the demand history and the associated fitted value for the history months, t=1 to 12.

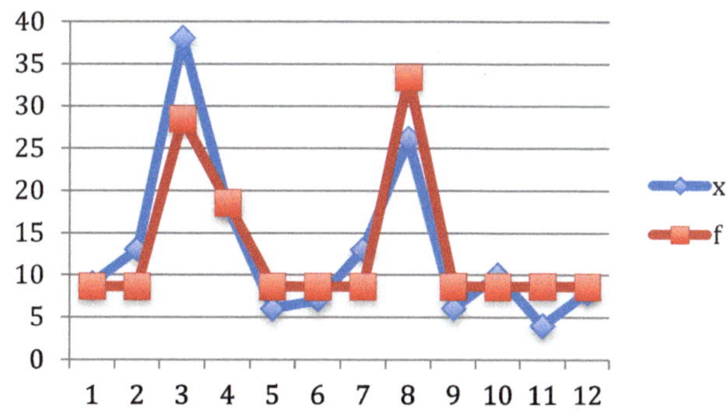

Fig. 6.1 Plot of demand history x(t), and fit f(t) for t=1 to 12

6.4 Standard Deviation and Cov

Continuing with Example 6.1, the sum of square of errors over the twelve history months is computed as:

$$\sum e(t)^2 = 224.86$$

So now, the standard deviation can be estimated as described earlier. This is,

$$s = \sqrt{224.86/10} = 4.742$$

The associated coefficient of variation becomes,

$$\text{cov} = s/a` = 4.742/8.621 = 0.550$$

6.5 Forecasts

The forecasts for the future months can now be generated. To apply, the analyst must have some projection of the promotion activity for the future months. In this model, p(τ) represents the portion of future month τ where a promo is to be held. Applying this data, the forecast is the following:

$$f(\tau) = a`+c`p(\tau) \quad \tau = 1,2,\ldots$$

Using the estimates of the coefficients from Example 6.1, the forecast model is,

$$f(\tau) = 8.621 + 49.59p(\tau) \quad \tau = 1,2,\ldots$$

Example 6.2 Applying the results from Example 6.1, suppose forecasts are needed for future months $\tau = 1, 2, 3$, where no promotion is planned for months 1 and 2, but a full month of promotion is set for month 3. Thereby, $p(1) = p(2) = 0$ and $p(3) = 1$. The forecasts for the first three future months become:

$$f(1) = 8.621$$
$$f(2) = 8.621$$
$$f(3) = 8.621 + 49.59 \times 1 = 58.52$$

6.6 Revision Stage

The second stage of the forecast model uses smoothing to estimate the coefficients of the model and pertains to the months beyond the initialize months. To apply this method, a smoothing parameter, α, is needed. At current month t, the data available to revise the coefficients are listed below:

$$t = \text{history month}$$
$$x(t) = \text{demand at month t}$$
$$p(t) = \text{promotion at month t}$$
$$a(t-1) = \text{estimate of the level coefficient at prior month } (t-1)$$
$$c(t-1) = \text{estimate of the promo coefficient at prior month } (t-1)$$
$$\alpha = \text{smoothing parameter}$$

Using the above data, the revise equations for the level, a(t), and for the promo, c(t), coefficients are the following:

$$a(t) = \alpha[x(t) - c(t-1)p(t)] + (1-\alpha)a(t-1)$$
$$\text{if } p(t) = 0, \text{set } c(t) = c(t-1), \text{ else,}$$
$$c(t) = \alpha[(x(t) - a(t))/p(t)] + (1-\alpha)c(t-1)$$

6.7 Unbiased Estimates

The expected values of the above two equations are listed below.

$$E[a(t)] = \alpha[a + c \times p(t) - c \times p(t)] + (1-\alpha)a = a$$
$$E[c(t)] = \alpha[(a + c \times p(t) - a)/p(t)] + (1-\alpha)c = c$$

Note where the expected value of a(t) is a (the true level), and for c(t) it is c (the true promo coefficient). This verifies that the revise equations yield unbiased estimators.

The revised coefficient estimates are then used to project unbiased forecasts for the future monthly demands.

Example 6.3 Continuing with Examples 6.1 and 6.2, suppose at the first future month, t=13, the new demand entry is x(13)=8 and there is no promotion. Hence, p(13)=0. In the example, the smoothing parameter is set as α=0.10. The revised coefficients and related computations are listed below:

$$a(13) = 0.1[8-0\times 49.59]+0.9[8.621] = 8.558$$
$$c(13) = 49.59$$
$$e(13) = [x(13)-f(13)] = [8-8.621] = -0.621$$
$$s(13) = \left\{0.1[-0.621]^2 + 0.9\left[4.742^2\right]\right\}^{0.5} = 4.501$$
$$cov(13) = s(13)/a(13) = 4.501/8.558 = 0.526$$

Continuing with the example, assume at month t=14, the demand is x(14)=2 and the promotion is p(14)=0. Thereby, the revised coefficients are:

$$a(14) = 0.1[2-0\times 49.59]+0.9[8.558] = 7.902$$
$$c(14) = 49.59$$

Going further at month t=15, suppose the demand is x(15)=67, and the month had a full promotion, whereby, p(14)=1.0. The revised estimates of the coefficients are the following;

$$a(15) = 0.1[67-1\times 49.59]+0.9[7.902] = 8.853$$
$$c(15) = 0.1[(67-8.853)/1.0]+0.9[49.594] = 50.450$$

The example continues for months t=13 to 24, with the associated demand, x(t), and promo, p(t), entries for each month listed in Table 6.3. The table also shows how the coefficients (a, c) and fitted values, f(t), would change as each month passes.

With each new month t, the computations described above are carried and the revised coefficients a(t) and c(t) become available. Hence, the forecasts for the future months, τ, become the following;

$$f(\tau) = a(t) + c(t)p(\tau) \quad \tau = 1,2,\ldots$$

At t=24, the forecast for future month τ is the following:

$$f(\tau) = 8.481 + 49.474p(\tau) \quad \tau = 1,2,\ldots$$

Table 6.3 Worksheet showing the demands x(t), and promotions p(t), for months t=13 to 24, and the corresponding estimates of the level a(t), the promo coefficient c(t), and the fitted value f(t)

t	x(t)	p(t)	a(t)	c(t)	f(t)
13	8	0	8.558	49.594	8.56
14	2	0	7.902	49.594	7.90
15	67	1	8.852	50.449	59.30
16	9	0	8.867	50.449	8.87
17	13	0	9.280	50.449	9.28
18	11	0	9.452	50.449	9.45
19	8	0	9.307	50.449	9.31
20	41	0.8	8.440	49.474	48.02
21	8	0	8.396	49.474	8.40
22	10	0	8.557	49.474	8.56
23	5	0	8.201	49.474	8.20
24	11	0	8.481	49.474	8.48

Assume now where forecasts are needed for each of the subsequent three months. Suppose also where marketing is planning no promo in future months $\tau=1$ and 2, but a 40% promotion in future month $\tau=3$. Thereby, p(1)=p(2)=0 and p(3)=0.4, and the associated forecasts are the following:

$$f(1) = 8.48$$

$$f(2) = 8.48$$

$$f(3) = 8.48 + 49.47(0.4) = 28.27$$

Figure 6.2 compares the total demand history, x(t), for the initialize months, with t=1 to 12 on the left-hand-side, and with the revised months, t=13 to 24 on the right-hand-side. The associated fitted values, f(t), are also shown.

6.8 Promotion Trend Model

Promotion forecasting is now extended to include a trend factor, and is here called the promotion trend model. The model pertains to demands that are trending, either up or down, in the long run, and has periodic promotion activities. The model is of the following form,

$$f(t) = a + bt + cp(t)$$

where f(t) is the fitted value for history month t, and p(t) is the promotion measure at month t. The coefficients are (a, b, c) where a is the intercept at t=0, b is the slope

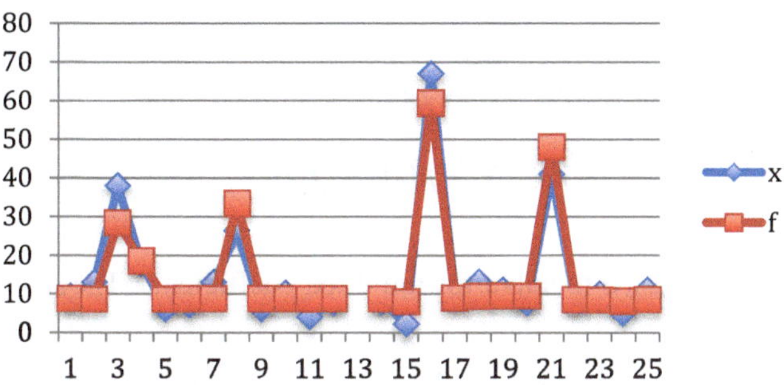

Fig. 6.2 Depiction of the demands (x) and the fitted values (f) for the12 history months (t=1 to 12), and for the subsequent 12 revised months (t=13 to 24)

coefficient, and c is the promo coefficient. As in the horizontal model, p(t) could be the portion of the month that contains promotion activity. As before, the model has two stages, initialize and revision. The initialize stage uses regression to estimate the coefficients, and the revision stage uses smoothing.

6.9 Initialize Stage

The initialize first stage requires some history data for the part. The data comes from the most recent N months of demand and promotion history. The history months are t=1,…., N. The demand history is x(1),…, x(N), and the promotion history is p(1),…, p(N). Regression analysis is used to estimate the coefficients for the level and promotion.

Using the least squares method in the typical way, the following three equations are generated to obtain the three unknowns, (a, b, c).

$$\Sigma x = (N)a + (\Sigma t)b + (\Sigma p)c$$
$$\Sigma xt = (\Sigma t)a + (\Sigma t^2)b + (\Sigma pt)c$$
$$\Sigma xp = (\Sigma p)a + (\Sigma pt)b + (\Sigma p^2)c$$

For notational ease, the summations listed above are abbreviations as shown below:

$$\sum_{t=1}^{N} x(t) = \Sigma x$$
$$\sum_{t=1}^{N} x(t)p(t) = \Sigma xp$$
$$\sum_{t=1}^{N} x(t)t = \Sigma xt$$
$$\sum_{t=1}^{N} p(t)t = \Sigma pt$$
$$\sum_{t=1}^{N} t = \Sigma t$$

$$\sum_{t=1}^{N} t^2 = \Sigma t^2$$
$$\sum_{t=1}^{N} p(t) = \Sigma p$$
$$\sum_{t=1}^{N} p(t)^2 = \sum p^2$$

Matrix methods are used to solve for the three coefficients. The matrix relation is the following:

$$\begin{bmatrix} \Sigma x \\ \Sigma xt \\ \Sigma xp \end{bmatrix} = \begin{bmatrix} N & \Sigma t & \Sigma p \\ \Sigma t & \Sigma t^2 & \Sigma pt \\ \Sigma p & \Sigma pt & \Sigma p^2 \end{bmatrix} \begin{bmatrix} a \\ b \\ c \end{bmatrix}$$

The following notation is now helpful. The vector, X becomes,

$$X = \begin{bmatrix} \Sigma x \\ \Sigma xt \\ \Sigma xp \end{bmatrix}$$

Matrix T is,

$$T = \begin{bmatrix} N & \Sigma t & \Sigma p \\ \Sigma t & \Sigma t^2 & \Sigma pt \\ \Sigma p & \Sigma pt & \Sigma p^2 \end{bmatrix}$$

and vector A is,

$$A = \begin{bmatrix} a \\ b \\ c \end{bmatrix}$$

Using the notation above, the relation below becomes,

$$X = TA$$

and the solution of the vector A is found as follows:

$$A = T^{-1}X$$

where T^{-1} is the inverse of the matrix T. For notational ease, the coefficient estimates are listed as: a`, b`, c`.

The fitted value for history month t is the following:

$$f(t) = a` + b`t + c`p(t) \quad t = 1 \text{ to } T$$

and the associated residual error is computed as below:

$$e(t) = x(t) - f(t)$$

6.10 Standard Deviation and Cov

To compute an estimate of the standard deviation of the forecast error, denoted as s, the sum of square of errors, $\sum e(t)^2$, is needed. With N months of history, the estimate of the standard deviation is computed as below:

$$s = \sqrt{\sum e(t)^2 / (N-3)}$$

Finally, the coefficient of variation uses the standard deviation, s, and the level, a, as follows:

$$cov = s/a`$$

Example 6.4 Assume the trend promotion forecast model will be used for a part with 12 months of past history of demands, x(t), and promotion, p(t), as listed in Table 6.4.

To begin, the summations needed to estimate the coefficients, (a, b, c), are tallied and the summations are below:

$$\sum x = 208$$
$$\sum xp = 35.6$$
$$\sum xt = 1384$$
$$\sum pt = 6$$
$$\sum t = 78$$
$$\sum t^2 = 650$$
$$\sum p = 1.1$$
$$\sum p^2 = 0.45$$

Applying the matrix notation given earlier, X and T become,

$$X = \begin{bmatrix} 208 \\ 1384 \\ 35.6 \end{bmatrix}$$

Table 6.4 Data for Example 6.4: history months t, demand history x(t), and promotion history p(t) for t = 1 to 12

t	x(t)	p(t)
1	8	0
2	10	0
3	38	0.4
4	22	0.2
5	11	0
6	10	0
7	10	0
8	32	0.5
9	15	0
10	10	0
11	26	0
12	16	0

$$T=\begin{bmatrix} 12 & 78 & 1.1 \\ 78 & 650 & 6 \\ 1.1 & 6 & 0.45 \end{bmatrix}$$

The inverse of the matrix T is the following;

$$T^{-1}=\begin{bmatrix} 0.440 & -0.049 & -0.423 \\ -0.049 & 0.007 & 0.024 \\ -0.423 & 0.024 & 2.942 \end{bmatrix}$$

Solving for the vector A, the coefficient estimates become,

$$a` = 8.645$$
$$b` = 0.350$$
$$c` = 49.967$$

Note, a` is an estimate for t = 0, and b` and c` are estimates for any month t = 1 to 12. Using the notation a(t), b(t) and c(t) as the estimates for month t,

$$a(0) = a`,\ b(12) = b`,\ c(12) = c`,\ \text{and}\ a(12) = a(0) + 12b`$$

So now, a(12) is the estimate of the level at the most current month.

Table 6.5 Worksheet with history months t, demand history x(t), promotion history p(t), fit f(t), and residual error e(t) for months t = 1 to 12

t	x(t)	p(t)	f(t)	e(t)
1	8	0	9.00	−0.99
2	10	0	9.35	0.66
3	38	0.4	29.68	8.32
4	22	0.2	20.04	1.96
5	11	0	10.40	0.61
6	10	0	10.75	−0.74
7	10	0	11.10	−1.10
8	32	0.5	36.43	−4.43
9	15	0	11.80	3.21
10	10	0	12.15	−2.15
11	26	0	12.50	13.51
12	16	0	12.85	3.16

Using the matrix solution results, the coefficients are the following:

$$a(12) = (a` + 12b`) = (8.645 + 12 \times 0.350) = 12.845$$
$$b(12) = b` = 0.350$$
$$c(12) = c` = 49.967$$

The fitted values for months t = 1 to 12 are obtained by the relation below:

$$f(t) = 8.645 + 0.350t + 49.967p(t) \quad t = 1 \text{ to } 12$$

The associated residual errors, e(t) = x(t)—f(t), can now be calculated for each of the history months. Table 6.5 is a list of the 12 history months, along with their demands, promotions, fitted values and residual errors.

The sum of squares of the $N = 12$ residuals errors is tallied and becomes,

$$\sum e(t)^2 = 303.386$$

This sum is needed to compute the estimate of the standard deviation, s, of the residual errors. The result is below:

$$s = \sqrt{303.386/9} = 5.806$$

So now, the coefficient of variation is calculated as follows:

$$cov = s/a(12) = 5.806/12.85 = 0.452$$

Figure 6.3 gives a comparison of the demands, x(t), and the fitted values, f(t), for the history months, t = 1 to 13.

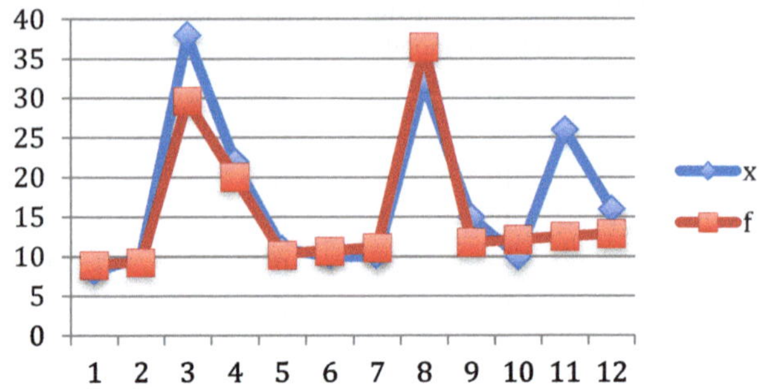

Fig. 6.3 Plot of history months t=1 to12, demands x(t), and fit f(t)

6.11 Revision Stage

The second stage of the promotion trend model is run beyond the initial 12 history months. This is when new demand and promotion data become available. With each new month of data, smoothing is used to revise the forecast coefficients, a, b and c. To apply this method, a smoothing parameter, α, is needed. At current month t, the data available to revise the coefficients are listed below:

$$t = \text{current month}$$
$$x(t) = \text{demand at month } t$$
$$a(t-1) = \text{estimate of the level at prior month } t-1$$
$$b(t-1) = \text{estimate of the slope at prior month } t-1$$
$$c(t-1) = \text{estimate of the promo coefficient at month } t-1$$
$$\alpha = \text{smooth parameter}$$

Using the above data, smoothing is used as shown below:

$$a(t) = \alpha[x(t) - c(t-1)p(t)] + (1-\alpha)[a(t-1) + b(t-1)]$$
$$b(t) = \alpha[a(t) - a(t-1)] + (1-\alpha)b(t-1)$$
$$\text{if } p(t) = 0,\ c(t) = c(t-1), \text{ else,}$$
$$c(t) = \alpha[(x(t) - a(t)) / p(t)] + (1-\alpha)c(t-1)$$

6.12 Unbiased Estimates

The expected values of the three coefficients, a(t), b(t) and c(t) are obtained below.

$$E[a(t)] = \alpha[a + c \times p(t) - c \times p(t)] + (1-\alpha)[a - b + b] = a$$
$$E[b(t)] = \alpha[a - (a - b)] + (1-\alpha)b = b$$
$$E[c(t)] = \alpha[(a + c \times p(t) - a) / p(t)] + (1-\alpha)c = c$$

Note where the expected value of a(t) is a, (the true level), b(t)=b, (the true slope), and for c(t), it is c (the true promo coefficient). This verifies that the revise equations yield unbiased estimators. The revised coefficient estimates are then used to project unbiased forecasts of future monthly demands.

Continuing with the Example 6.4, at t=12, the coefficients are the following:

$$a(12) = 12.845$$
$$b(12) = 0.350$$
$$c(12) = 49.967$$

Example 6.5 Suppose at month t=13, the demand is x(13)=30 and there is no promotion, p(13)=0. With this new data, the revise computations are below:

$$a(13) = 0.1[30 - 0 \times 49.9679] + 0.9[12.845 + 0.350] = 14.878$$
$$b(13) = 0.1(14.878 - 12.845) + 0.9(0.350) = 0.518$$
$$c(13) = 49.967$$
$$f(13) = 14.878 + 0 = 14.878$$

The associated residual error, estimate of the standard deviation and the coefficient of variation are computed as follows:

$$e(13) = [x(13)] - f`(13)]$$
$$= [30 - 14.878] = 15.122$$

$$s(13) = [\alpha \times e(13)^2 + (1-\alpha) \times s(12)^2]^{0.5}$$
$$= \left[0.1(15.122)^2 + 0.9\left(5.806^2\right)\right]^{0.5} = 6.181$$

$$cov(13) = s(13)/a(13) = 6.18/14.878 = 0.415$$

Continuing with the example, suppose at month t=14, the demand is x(14)=77, and a full promotion takes place, whereby p(14)=1.00. The revise computations for the coefficients are the following:

$$a(14) = 0.1[77 - 1.00 \times 49.968] + 0.9 \times [14.835] = 16.55$$
$$b(t) = 0.1[16.55 - 14.83] + 0.9 \times [0.514] = 0.63$$
$$c(14) = 0.1[(77 - 16.550)/1.00] + 0.9 \times [49.967] = 51.01$$

Table 6.6 Worksheet showing the months t = 13 to 24, the demands x(t), promotion p(t), and estimates of the level a(t), slope b(t), promo coefficient c(t), and the fit f(t)

t	x(t)	p(t)	a(t)	b(t)	c(t)	f(t)
13	30	0	14.875	0.52	49.97	14.88
14	77	1	16.557	0.63	51.01	66.52
15	26	0	18.072	0.72	51.01	18.07
16	12	0	18.115	0.65	51.01	18.12
17	28	0	19.693	0.75	51.01	19.69
18	31	0	21.496	0.85	51.01	21.50
19	21	0	22.213	0.84	51.01	22.21
20	32	0	23.947	0.93	51.01	23.95
21	24	0	24.788	0.92	51.01	24.79
22	34	0	26.537	1.00	51.01	26.54
23	23	0	27.085	0.96	51.01	27.09
24	32	0	28.438	1.00	51.01	28.44

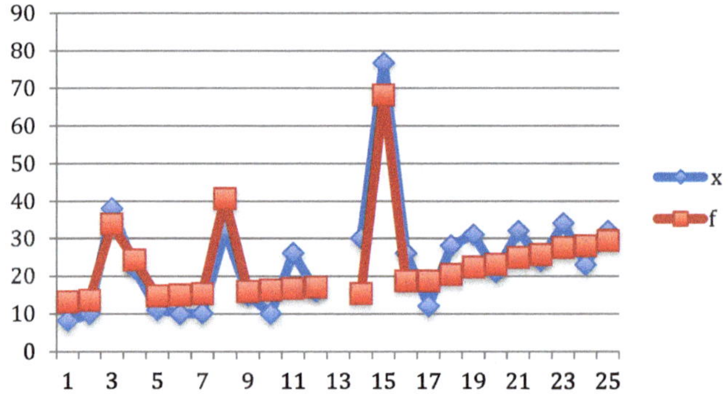

Fig. 6.4 Depiction of the history demands x(t), and their fit f(t), for history months 1 to 12 on the left, and for months 13 to 24 on the right

Table 6.6 is a list of the demands, x(t), and promotions, p(t), that are assumed for months t = 13 to 24. The table also gives the associated estimates of the coefficients, (a, b, c), and the fitted value, f(t), for each month t.

Note, during the revise months, the only promotion occurs at t = 14 which is for a full month and thereby, p(14) = 1.00.

Figure 6.4 depicts the demands, x(t), for the initial stage (t = 1 to 12), and for revision stage (t = 13 to 24), and also shows the corresponding fitted values, f(t) for each of the months.

Summary

Two promotion forecast models are described: the promotion horizontal model and the promotion trend model. Both have two stages; the initial stage and the revision stage. The initial stage uses N prior months of demand and promotion activities to estimate the coefficients of the model. The revision stage is for the months after the initial stage and uses the current demand and promotion data to update the forecast coefficients. Regression is used in the initial stage, and smoothing in the revision stage. In both situations, the standard deviation estimate and the coefficient of variation are computed.

Chapter 7
Multi-SKU Forecasts

7.1 Introduction

An sku is an abbreviation for the term stock-keeping-unit that identifies an item being in the inventory at a stocking location. Could be a part number, a product number, a style number, so forth. Should a model of a certain tool be in stock at a dealer, it is an sku at that dealer. If the same model is in stock in 1000 dealers, it is an sku in each of the 1000 dealers. It is also an sku at each distribution center that stocks the model. A truck parts dealer typically has 15,000 skus and a truck distribution center may have 100,000 skus. A shoe store in the mall may have 2000 skus in shoes alone, since each style by size and width is a separate sku. Forecasts are needed for each sku (usually monthly) to use in the inventory stocking computations.

When a part is stocked as a service part in an inventory system with five distribution centers (DC), the part is an sku in each of the DC's. Forecasts are needed for each part by location to arrange for the proper stock at each location. A forecast is also needed for the aggregate demands of the part in all locations so economic replenishments of the part from the supplier can be determined.

Consider a style shoe with 36 size and width combinations. Each size and width for the style shoe is an sku. Forecasts are needed for each size and width to be used in the inventory decisions at the distribution centers and at each store. The forecast is typically generated for the style itself, and this forecast is apportioned down to each of the size and width combinations. The same scenario also occurs in clothing, like men's shirts, with different size and widths, and so forth.

This chapter describes two common ways to forecast when multiple skus are of concern in an inventory system, the top-down method and the bottom-up method. Top-down is when the aggregate demand history is used to forecast the demands over the future months. The aggregate forecast is then allocated down to each sku using an sku percent representing it's portion of the total demand. This way, the forecasts for the total and for each sku are generated in a systematic manner. The

N. T. Thomopoulos, *Demand Forecasting for Inventory Control*,
DOI 10.1007/978-3-319-11976-2_7

Table 7.1 Location j demands x(j,t), and total demand x(t), at month t

t	x(1,t)	x(2,t)	x(3,t)	x(t)
1	1	1	5	7
2	4	3	3	10
3	0	3	7	10
4	1	3	3	7
5	4	6	3	13
6	1	2	9	12
7	0	3	13	16
8	2	3	10	15
9	5	7	1	13
10	3	6	5	14
11	1	3	11	15
12	0	8	8	16
13	4	7	3	14
14	2	6	10	18
15	3	8	6	17

bottom-up method is in use when a forecast is generated for each sku and the sum of the sku forecasts is used to determine the forecast for the total.

In both methods, the standard deviation of each forecast is of need for subsequent use in inventory decisions. Methods are shown on how to compute the standard deviations for each sku and for the total when the top-down and bottom-up methods are in use.

Example 7.1 Consider an inventory system with M=3 locations, denoted as: j=1, 2, 3, where they could represent three distribution centers, or three stores. Assume an item in stock has month 1 demands of one piece each for locations j=1 and j=2, and five pieces for location j=3. The notation for demands at location j in month t is denoted as x(j,t), and the total demand for all three locations is noted as x(t). Hence, the location demands in month 1 become: x(1,1)=1, x(2,1)=1, x(3,1)=5, and the total demand is x(1)=7. Table 7.1 lists the location and total demand for each of the first 15 months of history.

7.2 SKU Mean and Standard Deviation

In this chapter, the demands of an item at each location j are tallied separately and summed to yield the total demand as described in Example 7.1. In some of the forecasting methods, the known values for an item are the forecast of the total demand, F, the associated standard deviation, s, and also the percent of the total demand, p, that occurs at a particular sku. Of concern here is to use this information to estimate the forecast and standard deviation for an individual sku. A mathematical derivation of this situation follows.

Below shows how to compute the mean and an estimate of the standard deviation for an individual sku when the known values are the total mean, μ, and standard deviation, σ, for all skus combined. For convenience here, the demand for all skus is denoted as n and the demand for a selected sku is x. Further, p is the probability an arbitrary demand is for the selected sku. This way, with the parameters, n and p, x is almost distributed by the binomial distribution. But in this scenario, n is a random variable itself with mean μ and variance σ^2, and thereby, the binomial does not exactly apply. Below shows how to derive the mean and variance for the sku demand, x, when the data, (μ, σ, p), is provided.

7.3 Derivation of Binomial When n is a Random Variable

Suppose x is binomial with probability p, and n trials where, the number of trials, is a random variable with mean and variance as below:

$$E(n) = \mu$$

$$V(n) = \sigma^2$$

The mean and variance of x, labeled as E(x) and V(x) are obtained as below. Using conditional probability notation:

$$E(x \mid n) = np$$

$$E(x) = E(n)p = \mu p$$

$$V(x \mid n) = E(x^2 \mid n) - E(x \mid n)^2 = np(1-p)$$

$$E(x^2 \mid n) = V(x \mid n) + E(x \mid n)^2 = p(1-p)n + p^2 n^2$$

$$\begin{aligned} E\left(x^2\right) &= p(1-p)E(n) + p^2 E\left(n^2\right) \\ &= p(1-p)\mu + p^2\left(\mu^2 + \sigma^2\right) \end{aligned}$$

$$V(x) = E(x^2) - E(x)^2 = p(1-p)\,\mu + p^2\,\sigma^2$$

In summary,

$$E(x) = p\,\mu$$

$$V(x) = p(1-p)\,\mu + p^2\,\sigma^2$$

7.4 Top-Down Forecasting Method

Top-down forecasting involves the following seven steps:

1. Gather N months of demand history for each sku,

$$x(j, t) \qquad j = 1 \text{ to } M \text{ and } t = 1 \text{ to } N.$$

2. Sum the sku demands by month to yield the total monthly demands,

$$x(t) = \Sigma x(j, t) \qquad j = 1 \text{ to } M, t = 1 \text{ to } N.$$

3. Using the total monthly demands, generate the forecasts for the future months,

$$f(\tau) \quad \tau = 1, 2,$$

4. Compute an estimate of the standard deviation of the 1 month ahead forecast error, s.
5. Measure the portion of total demand that applies to sku j,

$$p(j) = \Sigma x(j, t) / \Sigma x(t) \qquad j = 1 \text{to} M$$

6. Allocate the total monthly forecasts to each sku,

$$f(j, \tau) = p(j) f(\tau) \qquad j = 1 \text{ to } M, \ \tau = 1, \ 2,$$

7. Calculate an estimate of the standard deviation for each sku,

$$s(j) = [a \times p(j)(1 - p(j)) + (p(j) \times s)^2]^{0.5} \quad j = 1 \text{ to } M$$

where *a* is the level and *s* is an estimate of the standard deviation for the total forecast.

7.5 Total Demand Forecasts

Continuing with Example 7.1, the first step is to forecast the total demands one month at a time. When the part is new and has only one month of demand history, the trend smoothing model is applied with parameter values $\beta = 0.05$ for the slope, and the smoothing parameter, α, value for the level is as follows:

$$\alpha = \max(0.10, 1/t) \quad t = 1, 2, \ldots$$

Month-1 Forecast In month t=1, the computations are the following. Note, the prior values of the level and slope, at t=0, are a(0)=b(0)=0.00, since the part is new. The total demand for the part is x(1)=7, and the parameters are α=max(0.10, 1/1)=1.00 and β=0.05. Thereby, the smoothed values of the level and the slope become:

$$\begin{aligned} a(1) &= \alpha x(1) + (1-\alpha)\left[a(0) + b(0)\right] \\ &= 1.00 \times 7 + (1-1.00) \times 0 = 7.00 \end{aligned}$$

$$\begin{aligned} b(1) &= \beta\left[a(1) - a(0)\right] + (1-\beta)b(0) \\ &= 0.05(7.00 - 0.00) + 0.95 \times 0.00 = 0.35 \end{aligned}$$

The 1-month ahead forecast becomes:

$$\begin{aligned} f(1) &= a(1) + b(1) \times 1 \\ &= 7.00 + 0.35 \times 1 = 7.35 \end{aligned}$$

Since the part is new, the prior standard deviation estimate is s(0)=0.00 and the revised standard deviation becomes,

$$\begin{aligned} s(1) &= \left\{\alpha\left[x(1) - a(0)\right]^2 + (1-\alpha)s(0)^2\right\}^{0.5} \\ &= \left\{1.00\left[7.00 - 0.00\right]^2 + 0.00 \times 0\right\}^{0.5} = 7.00 \end{aligned}$$

The coefficient of variation is below:

$$\begin{aligned} cov(1) &= s(1) / a(1) \\ &= 7.00 / 7.00 = 1.00 \end{aligned}$$

These are the values listed in Table 7.1 for the first month (t=1) of demand history.

Month-2 Forecast Continuing with Example 7,1, the corresponding computations for month t=2, become: α=max(0.10, ½)=0.50, β=0.05, x(2)=10, a(1)=8.68, b(2)=0.42, f=9.09, s(2)=5.29 and cov(2)=0.61. These values are in Table 7.2 when t=2.

Month-t Forecast Table 7.2 is a listing of the forecasting results for the total demand for each of the months t=1 to 15.

7.6 Location Portion of Demand

Consider month t=1 again where the demands are 1, 1 and 5 for locations 1, 2 and 3, respectively. The portion of demand for each location becomes:

$$p(1) = 1/7 = 0.142$$

Table 7.2 Worksheet for total forecasts with months t, monthly demands x(t), level a(t), slope b(t), 1 month ahead forecast f(t), standard deviation s(t), and coefficient of variation cov(t)

t	x(t)	a(t)	b(t)	f(t)	s(t)	cov(t)
1	7	7.00	0.35	7.35	7.00	1.00
2	10	8.68	0.42	9.09	5.29	0.61
3	10	9.39	0.43	9.83	4.35	0.46
4	7	9.12	0.40	9.52	4.03	0.44
5	13	10.21	0.43	10.64	3.92	0.38
6	12	10.87	0.44	11.31	3.62	0.33
7	16	11.98	0.48	12.46	3.79	0.32
8	15	12.77	0.49	13.27	3.66	0.29
9	13	13.24	0.49	13.73	3.45	0.26
10	14	13.75	0.49	14.25	3.28	0.24
11	15	14.32	0.50	14.82	3.12	0.22
12	16	14.93	0.50	15.44	2.98	0.20
13	14	15.29	0.49	15.79	2.87	0.19
14	18	16.01	0.51	16.51	2.81	0.18
15	17	16.56	0.51	17.07	2.67	0.16

$$p(2) = 1/7 = 0.142$$

$$p(3) = 5/7 = 0.714$$

At month t=2, the cumulative demand for each of the three locations are: 5, 4 and 8 at j=1, 2, 3, respectively. The cumulative total demand is 17. Hence, the portion of demands for each location becomes:

$$p(1) = 5/17 = 0.294$$

$$p(2) = 4/17 = 0.235$$

$$p(2) = 8/17 = 0.471$$

These are the values at t=2.

In the same way, the location portion of the total demand by month is calculated as each month passes by. The values for months 1–15 are shown in the Table 7.3.

7.7 The Level by Location and Total

The level for the total demand at month t is denoted as a(t), and the level for location j at t is a(j,t). In the example, at month t=1, the level for the total monthly demand was reported as a(1)=7.00, and the corresponding level for each location j becomes:

Table 7.3 Monthly portion of demand p(j), by location j

t	p(1)	p(2)	p(3)
1	0.14	0.14	0.71
2	0.29	0.24	0.47
3	0.19	0.26	0.56
4	0.18	0.29	0.53
5	0.21	0.34	0.45
6	0.19	0.31	0.51
7	0.15	0.28	0.57
8	0.14	0.27	0.59
9	0.17	0.30	0.52
10	0.18	0.32	0.50
11	0.17	0.30	0.53
12	0.15	0.32	0.53
13	0.16	0.34	0.50
14	0.16	0.34	0.51
15	0.16	0.35	0.49

$$a(1,1) = p(1)a(1) = 0.142 \times 7 = 1.00$$

$$a(2,1) = p(2)a(1) = 0.142 \times 7 = 1.00$$

$$a(3,1) = p(3)a(1) = 0.741 \times 7 = 5.00$$

Table 7.4 lists the level for the total and for each location for every month t = 1 to 15.

7.8 Standard Deviation by Location and Total

The estimate of the standard deviation for the total demand at month t is denoted as s(t), and the same value for location j is s(j,t). The location standard deviations are calculated as shown earlier. At month t = 1, s(1) = 7.00 and for j = 1,

$$s(1,1) = \left[7.00\{0.142(1-0.142)\} + (0.142 \times 7.00)^2\right]^{0.5} = 1.36$$

In the same way, the standard deviation estimates for locations j = 2 and 3 are s(2,1) = 0.136 and s(3,1) = 5.14. Table 7.5 lists the standard deviations for month t = 1 to 15 for the total demand and for each of the three locations.

Table 7.4 Monthly estimates of total level a(t), and location j level a(j,t)

t	a(t)	a(1,t)	a(2,t)	a(3,t)
1	7.00	1.00	1.00	5.00
2	8.68	2.55	2.04	4.08
3	9.39	1.74	2.44	5.22
4	9.12	1.61	2.68	4.83
5	10.21	2.17	3.48	4.56
6	10.87	2.03	3.32	5.53
7	11.98	1.76	3.35	6.87
8	12.77	1.85	3.41	7.52
9	13.24	2.31	3.98	6.94
10	13.75	2.47	4.35	6.94
11	14.32	2.39	4.34	7.59
12	14.93	2.22	4.84	7.87
13	15.29	2.45	5.19	7.65
14	16.01	2.49	5.42	8.09
15	16.56	2.61	5.80	8.15

Table 7.5 Monthly estimates of the total standard deviation s(t), and location j standard deviation s(j,t)

t	s(t)	s(1,t)	s(2,t)	s(3,t)
1	7.00	1.36	1.36	5.14
2	5.29	2.06	1.76	2.89
3	4.35	1.44	1.75	2.86
4	4.03	1.35	1.82	2.61
5	3.92	1.55	2.02	2.37
6	3.62	1.45	1.88	2.47
7	3.79	1.35	1.88	2.77
8	3.66	1.36	1.86	2.78
9	3.45	1.51	1.97	2.57
10	3.28	1.54	2.01	2.48
11	3.12	1.50	1.98	2.51
12	2.98	1.44	2.05	2.49
13	2.87	1.51	2.09	2.42
14	2.81	1.51	2.12	2.45
15	2.67	1.54	2.15	2.42

7.9 Cov by Location and Total

The coefficient of variation for the total demand at month t is denoted as cov(t), and for location j it is cov(j,t). At month t=1,

$$cov(1) = s(1) / a(1) = 7 / 7 = 1.00$$

$$cov(1,1) = 1.36 / 1.00 = 1.36$$

$$cov(2,1) = 1.36 / 1.00 = 1.36$$

$$cov(3,1) = 5.14 / 5.00 = 1.03$$

In the same way, the cov's are computed as each month t passes by. Table 7.6 gives the progress of the covs for the total and for each location for months t=1 to 15.

7.10 Bottom-Up Forecasting Method

Bottom-up forecasting requires the following five steps.

1. Gather the N most recent history demands by sku j.

$$x(j,t) = 1 \text{ to } M \text{ and } t = 1 \text{ to } N$$

2. Generate the forecast for each sku j for future months τ.

$$f(j,\tau) \quad j = 1 \text{ to } M \text{ and } \tau = 1, 2, \ldots$$

3. Compute the standard deviation estimate for each sku j as of the current time t.

$$s(j,t) \qquad j = 1 \text{ to } M$$

4. Sum all the sku forecasts to yield the total forecast.

$$f(\tau) = \Sigma f(j,\tau) \qquad j = 1 \text{ to } M \text{ and } \tau = 1, 2, \ldots$$

5. Compute the standard deviation estimate for the total demand, s.

Table 7.6 Monthly measures of the coefficient of variationfor the total, cov(t), and for location j, cov(j,t)

t	cov(t)	cov(1,t)	cov(2,t)	cov(3,t)
1	1.00	1.36	1.36	1.03
2	0.61	0.81	0.86	0.71
3	0.46	0.83	0.72	0.55
4	0.44	0.84	0.68	0.54
5	0.38	0.71	0.58	0.52
6	0.33	0.72	0.57	0.45
7	0.32	0.77	0.56	0.40
8	0.29	0.74	0.55	0.37
9	0.26	0.65	0.49	0.37
10	0.24	0.62	0.46	0.36
11	0.22	0.63	0.46	0.33
12	0.20	0.65	0.42	0.32
13	0.19	0.61	0.40	0.32
14	0.18	0.61	0.39	0.30
15	0.16	0.59	0.37	0.30

7.11 Location j Forecasts

Example 7.2 Forecasts are required for each location j, using the most current demands and the associated parameters. Assume for this example, the trend smoothing model will be used with parameters, $\alpha = \max(0.10, 1/t)$ where t is the number of months of history, and the slope parameter is $\beta = 0.05$. Recall, the revised forecasts for any month t are obtained as follows:

$$a(j,t) = \alpha x(j,t) + (1-\alpha)\left[a(j,t-1) + b(j,t-1)\right]$$

$$b(j,t) = \beta\left[a(j,t) - a(j,t-1)\right] + (1-\beta)b(j,t-1)$$

and

$$f(j,\tau) = a(j,t) + b(j,t)\tau \qquad \tau = 1,2,\ldots$$

The standard deviation estimate for sku j and current month t, is revised in the following way:

$$s(j,t) = \left\{\alpha e(j,t)^2 + (1-\alpha)s(j,t-1)^2\right\}^{0.5}$$

where e(j,t) = x(j,t) − f(j,t − 1) is the 1 month ahead forecast error at month t. The coefficient of variation for sku j and month t becomes,

$$\text{cov(j,t)} = \text{s(j,t)} / \text{a(j,t)}$$

Forecasts at Location j = 1 At month t = 1, when the item is new, the demand for sku j is denoted as x(j,1). The prior estimates of the level and slope, at t = 0, are a(j,0) = 0 and b(j,0) = 0, respectively. The smoothed values of the level and the slope become,

$$\text{a}(1,1) = 1.00$$

$$\text{b}(1,1) = 0.05$$

and the τ-month ahead forecast becomes:

$$\text{f}(1,\tau) = 1.00 + 0.05\tau \qquad \tau = 1, 2, \ldots$$

The standard deviation estimate becomes:

$$\text{s}(1,1) = 1.00$$

and the cov is

$$\text{cov}(1,1) = 1.00$$

These are the values listed in Table 7.7 for the first month (t = 1) of demand history. The table also lists the forecast results for the months t = 1 to 15. Table 7.8 lists the corresponding results for location j = 2, and Table 7.9 gives the same for location j = 3.

7.12 Bottom-Up Total Forecast

The total forecast, at month t, using the bottom-up method is computed in the following way for a trend forecast model. First, the levels for each of the sku's are summed to give the level for the total demand as shown below:

$$\text{a(t)} = \sum_{j=1}^{M} a(j,t)$$

In the same way, the slopes from each sku j, are summed to yield the slope for the total demand,

$$b(\text{t}) = \sum_{j=1}^{M} b(j,t)$$

Table 7.7 Forecast worksheet for location 1 with months t, level a(1,t), slope b(1,t), forecast f(1,t), standard deviation s(1,t) and coefficient of variation cov(1,t)

t	x(1,t)	a(1,t)	b(1,t)	f(1,t)	s(1,t)	cov(1,t)
1	1	1.00	0.05	1.05	1.00	1.00
2	4	2.53	0.12	2.65	2.20	0.87
3	0	1.77	0.08	1.85	2.36	1.34
4	1	1.63	0.07	1.70	2.09	1.28
5	4	2.16	0.09	2.25	2.13	0.99
6	1	2.05	0.08	2.13	2.01	0.98
7	0	1.82	0.07	1.89	2.03	1.11
8	2	1.90	0.07	1.97	1.90	1.00
9	5	2.31	0.08	2.39	2.05	0.89
10	3	2.45	0.09	2.54	1.96	0.80
11	1	2.38	0.08	2.46	1.92	0.81
12	0	2.22	0.07	2.28	1.98	0.89
13	4	2.46	0.08	2.53	1.96	0.80
14	2	2.48	0.07	2.55	1.86	0.75
15	3	2.60	0.08	2.67	1.77	0.68

Table 7.8 Forecast worksheet for location 2 with months t, level a(2,t), slope b(2,t), forecast f(2,t), standard deviation s(2,t) and coefficient of variation cov(2,t)

t	x(2,t)	a(2,t)	b(2,t)	f(2,t)	s(2,t)	cov(2,t)
1	1	1.00	0.05	1.05	1.00	1.00
2	3	2.03	0.10	2.12	1.55	0.76
3	3	2.42	0.11	2.53	1.36	0.56
4	3	2.65	0.12	2.77	1.20	0.45
5	6	3.41	0.15	3.56	1.80	0.53
6	2	3.30	0.14	3.44	1.77	0.53
7	3	3.38	0.14	3.51	1.64	0.49
8	3	3.45	0.13	3.58	1.55	0.45
9	7	3.96	0.15	4.11	1.85	0.47
10	6	4.30	0.16	4.46	1.85	0.43
11	3	4.32	0.15	4.47	1.82	0.42
12	8	4.82	0.17	4.99	2.06	0.43
13	7	5.19	0.18	5.38	2.05	0.39
14	6	5.44	0.18	5.62	1.96	0.36
15	8	5.86	0.20	6.06	2.00	0.34

So now, the forecast for the τ-th future month for the total demand as of the current month t is the following:

$$f(\tau) = a(t) + b(t)\tau \qquad \tau = 1, 2, \ldots$$

Table 7.9 Forecast worksheet for location 3 with months t, level a(3,t), slope b(3,t), forecast f(3,t), standard deviation s(3,t) and coefficient of variation cov(3,t)

t	x(3,t)	a(3,t)	b(3,t)	f(3,t)	s(3,t)	cov(3,t)
1	5	5.00	0.25	5.25	5.00	1.00
2	3	4.13	0.19	4.32	3.88	0.94
3	7	5.21	0.24	5.45	3.52	0.68
4	3	4.84	0.21	5.05	3.29	0.68
5	3	4.64	0.19	4.82	3.08	0.66
6	9	5.52	0.22	5.74	3.29	0.60
7	13	6.78	0.27	7.05	4.10	0.60
8	10	7.42	0.29	7.71	3.97	0.54
9	1	6.97	0.26	7.22	4.36	0.63
10	5	7.00	0.24	7.24	4.20	0.60
11	11	7.62	0.26	7.88	4.16	0.55
12	8	7.89	0.26	8.16	3.94	0.50
13	3	7.64	0.24	7.88	4.08	0.53
14	10	8.09	0.25	8.34	3.93	0.49
15	6	8.11	0.24	8.34	3.80	0.47

The 1 month ahead forecast error is

$$e(t) = x(t) - f(t-1)$$

and the revised standard deviation estimate becomes

$$s(t) = \sqrt{\alpha e(t)^2 + (1-\alpha)s(t-1)^2}$$

Finally, the coefficient of variation is

$$cov(t) = s(t) / a(t)$$

7.13 Total Forecast at Month 1

At month t = 1, the level and slope are obtained from the same values for the three locations as follows:

$$a(1) = 1.00 + 1.00 + 5.00 = 7.00$$

$$b(1) = 0.05 + 0.05 + 0.15 = 0.25$$

Hence, the forecast of the total demand for future month τ is

$$f(\tau) = 7.00 + 0.25\tau \qquad \tau = 1, 2, ...$$

Table 7.10 Forecast worksheet for the total with months t, level a(t), slope b(t), forecast f(t), standard deviation s(t), and coefficient of variation cov(t)

t	x(t)	a(t)	b(t)	f(t)	s(t)	cov(t)
1	7	7.00	0.35	7.35	7.00	1.00
2	10	8.68	0.42	9.09	5.29	0.61
3	10	9.39	0.43	9.83	4.35	0.46
4	7	9.12	0.40	9.52	4.03	0.44
5	13	10.21	0.43	10.64	3.92	0.38
6	12	10.87	0.44	11.31	3.62	0.33
7	16	11.98	0.48	12.46	3.79	0.32
8	15	12.77	0.49	13.27	3.66	0.29
9	13	13.24	0.49	13.73	3.45	0.26
10	14	13.75	0.49	14.25	3.28	0.24
11	15	14.32	0.50	14.82	3.12	0.22
12	16	14.93	0.50	15.44	2.98	0.20
13	14	15.29	0.49	15.79	2.87	0.19
14	18	16.01	0.51	16.51	2.81	0.18
15	17	16.56	0.51	17.07	2.67	0.16

The forecast error for month t=1 is e(1)=7.00−0.00=7.00
and so, the standard deviation estimate is:

$$s(1) = \left[1.00 \times (7^2) + 0 \times 0\right]^{0.5} = 7.00$$

Finally, the cov becomes,

$$\text{cov}(1) = 7.00 / 7.00 = 1.00$$

The values are listed in Table 7.10 at t=1.

In the same way, the corresponding forecasts and related measures are calculated and listed in the table for months t=1 to 15.

7.14 Horizontal SKU Forecasts

Sometimes there are many sku's where forecasts are needed on the the future demands. This happens often in consumer items where many sizes and or colors of styles are stocked in the inventory in the distribution centers or in stores where replenishment decisions are needed on each sku. In these situations, the demands over the short run are often of the horizontal type and the forecasts are generated on a top-down basis.

Table 7.11 Portion of demand by size, s, and width, w, p(s,w)

s/w	N	M	W
7	0.0094	0.0188	0.0102
8	0.0129	0.0259	0.0184
8.5	0.0165	0.0329	0.0267
9	0.0200	0.0400	0.0349
9.5	0.0235	0.0470	0.0431
10	0.0270	0.0541	0.0513
10.5	0.0055	0.0500	0.0550
11	0.0052	0.0470	0.0517
11.5	0.0049	0.0441	0.0485
12	0.0045	0.0412	0.0453
13	0.0042	0.0382	0.0420

In this section, the example to illustrate the method is taken from the shoe industry where a style shoe is under review and the style has many combinations by size and width. In a top-down manner, the demand history of the style is used to forecast the style forecasts for the future months. The style forecast is then allocated to each size and width combination via a measure of the prior demand for each sku.

In the shoe industry, the portion of demand by sku is called a profile and the profile is often the same for a whole class of styles. Caution however, the profile of men's work shoes may be different than the profile of men's dress shoes. The profile could also change by location of the country where, for casual shoes, the profile in Florida may be different than the profile in Minnesota, say. The profile may even be different by store location in a city where the store is in an ethnic neighborhood. Some ethnic men may be larger in general than other ethnic men.

Example 7.3 Assume a style shoe has 33 sku's as identified in Table 7.11. The sizes range from 7.0 to 13.0 and the widths are narrow (N), medium (M) and wide (W). For the style of interest, the portion of total demand by sku is also listed in the table. The sum over all of the sku portions, p(s,w), is 1.000.

7.15 SKU Forecasts at the Distribution Center

Forecasts are needed at the distribution center and at each store. The forecasts at the DC is used to determine the replenish needs for each size and width. When new stock is needed, the DC places an order by sku with the plant that serves as the source supplier. The example assumes the monthly forecast for the style is F=500 pair. Using the style forecast, F, the associated sku forecast for the DC is generated by,

$$f(s,w) = p(s,w) \times F$$

Table 7.12 Raw forecast for total demand f(s,w) by size s, and width w, when F=500 per month at the distribution center

s/w	N	M	W
7	4.70	9.41	5.10
8	6.47	12.94	9.21
8.5	8.23	16.46	13.33
9	10.00	19.99	17.44
9.5	11.76	23.52	21.56
10	13.52	27.05	25.67
10.5	2.75	24.99	27.49
11	2.59	23.52	25.87
11.5	2.43	22.05	24.25
12	2.26	20.58	22.64
13	2.10	19.11	21.02

Table 7.13 Integer forecast x(s,w) by size s, and width w, of F=500 at the distribution center

s/w	N	M	W
7	5	9	5
8	6	13	9
8.5	8	16	13
9	10	20	17
9.5	12	24	22
10	14	27	26
10.5	3	25	27
11	3	24	26
11.5	2	22	24
12	2	21	23
13	2	19	21

The raw forecasts are rounded to integers. Because of rounding, the sum of the raw forecasts will not always equal the corresponding sum of the integer forecasts.

Consider sku s=10 and w=M, where p(10,M)=0.0541, the raw forecast for this sku is,

$$f(10, M) = 0.0541 \times 500 = 27.05$$

The raw forecasts are listed in Table 7.12 and the corresponding integer forecasts are in Table 7.13. The raw forecast for size s=7 and width w=N, say, becomes,

f(7,N)=p(7,N) × F=0.0094 × 500=4.7. The corresponding integer forecast is f(7,N)=5 pair.

Table 7.14 Integer forecast x(s,w) by size s, and width w, when F=10 at a store location

s/w	N	M	W
7	0	0	0
8	0	0	0
8.5	0	0	0
9	0	0	0
9.5	0	0	0
10	0	1	1
10.5	0	0	1
11	0	0	1
11.5	0	0	0
12	0	0	0
13	0	0	0

Table 7.15 Integer forecast x(s,w) by size s, and width w, when F=20 at a store location

s/w	N	M	W
7	0	0	0
8	0	1	0
8.5	0	1	1
9	0	1	1
9.5	0	1	1
10	1	1	1
10.5	0	1	1
11	0	1	1
11.5	0	1	1
12	0	1	1
13	0	1	1

7.16 SKU Forecasts at the Stores

Suppose the forecast for a store is ten pair a month, F=10, for the style. The associated integer forecasts for the style size and width at the store become those listed in Table 7.14. Although the raw forecasts for this store sums to ten pair,

$$\Sigma\Sigma f(s,w) = 10$$

the corresponding integer forecasts sum to only four pair.

Table 7.15 lists the integer forecasts for a store when the monthly style forecast is F=20 pair. In this scenario, both the raw and the integer forecasts sum to 20 pair.

Table 7.16 Integer forecast x(s,w) by size s, and width w, when F=30 at a store location

s/w	N	M	W
7	0	1	0
8	0	1	1
8.5	0	1	1
9	1	1	1
9.5	1	1	1
10	1	2	2
10.5	0	1	2
11	0	1	2
11.5	0	1	1
12	0	1	1
13	0	1	1

Table 7.16 lists the forecasts when the style forecast is F=30 pair. In this situation, the sum of the raw forecasts is 30, but the sum of the integer forecasts is 28 pair.

Summary

The top-down and bottom-up forecasting methods are used when multiple skus are related in some manner, like the same part is stocked in various locations, or when a retail item is available in a variety of sizes, colors or models. Could be when a part (or product) is stocked in multiple locations, and forecasts at each location is needed as well as a forecast for the total. A common use is for retail items, shoes, shirts, sweaters, so forth, where forecasts are needed by each size and for the total. The top-down method first generates forecasts of the total demand, and second, this forecast is apportioned down to each sku. The bottom-up method applies when a forecast for each sku is generated and the sum of the forecasts is used for the total. The individual sku forecasts are needed for subsequent inventory computation decisions, and the total forecast is needed to arrange with the supplier the replenish needs for the total inventory system. In all situations, measures of the forecast error are needed for subsequent inventory decisions.

Chapter 8
Forecast Sensitivity

8.1 Introduction

Along the supply chain, in distribution centers, stores, dealers, so forth, forecasts are in continual need for inventory decisions to project the flow of demands over the future months for each item stocked. The more accurate the forecasts, the better the inventory decisions and the more profitable the entity. A 10 % decrease in the measure of the forecast error will result in approximately a 10+ percent decrease in the amount of safety stock needed. This reduced stock is very helpful to the profit margin on the inventory system.

In this chapter, a series of simulation runs are developed to apprise the forecaster on how some elements in forecasting affect the accuracy of the forecasts. For this purpose, the forecast accuracy is measured by the coefficient of variation, cov, of the 1-month ahead forecast error. A first series of tests concern the number of months of demand history to use in developing the forecasts. The cov is measured as the history of demands range from 6 to 48 months and the forecasts are for the horizontal and trend demand patterns. A second series of tests are aimed at measuring how forecast accuracy depends on the choice of parameters and forecast model selected. Three separate simulations are run; one for the horizontal demand pattern, another for the trend demand pattern, and yet another for the seasonal demand pattern. A third series of tests demonstrate how damaging outlier demands are to the forecasts and the forecast accuracy. Two examples are given, one for a horizontal demand pattern and another for a trend demand pattern.

8.2 Cov by NMH when Horizontal Demands and Forecasts

A simulation is run to determine how the accuracy of the forecast is affected as the number of months of history (NMH) varies when the demand pattern is horizontal and a horizontal forecast model is applied. In this simulation, the NMH of demand

N. T. Thomopoulos, *Demand Forecasting for Inventory Control*,
DOI 10.1007/978-3-319-11976-2_8

Table 8.1 Average cov from 25 samples by number of months history, NMH, using the horizontal moving average forecast model

NMH	Cov
6	0.362
12	0.346
18	0.297
24	0.292
30	0.303
36	0.316
42	0.320
48	0.318

history is randomly generated from a horizontal demand pattern where the individual monthly demands are normally distributed with a mean of μ and a standard deviation of $\sigma = \text{cov} \times \mu$ with $\text{cov} = 0.30$. The demands are denoted as, x(1),…, x(*N*), where N = NMH, and the average demand is computed by the sample average,

$$a` = [x(1) + \ldots + x(N)]/N$$

The forecast errors of the 12 future months are calculated by: $e(t) = (x(t) - a`)$ $t = N + 1$ to $N + 12$, and the standard deviation estimate is computed as,

$$s = \sqrt{\sum e(t)^2 / (N-1)}$$

So now, the coefficient of variation for this simulated sample is:

$$\text{cov} = s / a`$$

The simulation is carried out 25 times and the average cov for the stated NMH is computed.

Table 8.1 lists the average cov for each of the NMH's (6–48) selected in this simulation. Note, the cov reaches equilibrium when 18 months of history is used to estimate the average demand.

8.3 Cov by NMH when Trend Demands and Forecasts

A simulation is run to determine how the accuracy of the forecast changes when the number months of demand history varies for a trend demand pattern and a trend forecast model is in use. In this situation, NMH months of demand history is randomly generated from a trend demand pattern where the monthly demands are slowly ramping upwards. Each demand is normally distributed with a mean $\mu(\tau) = (a + bt)$ and the standard deviation is $\sigma(\tau)$, where $\sigma(\tau) = \text{cov} \times \mu(t)$, and

Table 8.2 Average cov from 25 samples by number of month history, NMH, using the trend regression forecast model

NMH	Cov
6	0.690
12	0.393
18	0.334
24	0.293
30	0.302
36	0.330
42	0.318
48	0.314

cov = 0.30. Because the mean of each month is slowly ramping up in this simulation, the associated standard deviation is also becoming larger with each month. The randomly generated demands are denoted as, x(1),…, x(N), where N=NMH.

The fit of the demands has two coefficients, (a, b), and these are estimated as follows:

$$b' = \left[\sum x \sum t - N \sum xt\right] / \left[\left(\sum t\right)^2 - N \sum t^2\right]$$

$$a' = \left[\sum x - b \sum t\right] / N$$

Where the summations range from t=1 to N, and for brevity, the summation notations are: $\sum x = \sum x(t)$ and $\sum xt = \sum x(t)t$

The forecast values for the 12 future months are computed by,

$$f(t) = a` + b`t \quad t = N+1 \text{ to } N+12$$

The average value of the forecast is here denoted as f`. The forecast errors of the 12 future months is obtained, e(t)=(x(t)−f(t)) t=N+1 to N+12, and the standard deviation estimate is computed as,

$$s = \sqrt{\sum e(t)^2 / (N-1)}$$

So now, the coefficient of variation for this simulated sample is

$$cov = s / f`$$

The simulation is carried out 25 times and the average cov for the stated NMH is computed.

Table 8.2 lists the average cov for each of the NMH's (6–48) selected in this simulation. Note, the cov reaches equilibrium when N=24 months of history are used to generate the forecasts. This result is influenced because the demands are created from a trend demand pattern and the associated forecasts are also generated from a trend forecast model.

Table 8.3 Average cov from 25 samples by discount forecast models, horizontal and trend, and parameter β when true demand pattern is horizontal

β	Cov(H)	Cov(T)
0.95	0.333	0.438
0.90	0.334	0.445
0.85	0.336	0.457
0.80	0.338	0.474
0.75	0.341	0.499
0.70	0.345	0.531

8.4 Cov by Parameter and Forecast Model when Horizontal Demands

In this simulation, the accuracy of the forecast is measured when the demands are from a horizontal demand pattern and the forecasts are from the discount forecast models of horizontal and trend and the discount parameters vary. For this purpose, 24 months of demand history are randomly generated from a horizontal demand pattern where the individual monthly demands are normally distributed with a mean of μ and a standard error of $\sigma = \text{cov} \times \mu$ with cov = 0.300. The demands are denoted as, x(1),…, x(24).

The forecasts are generated by the horizontal discount model and also by the trend discount model. The models use one parameter denoted as β. The values of β are: (0.95, 0.90, 0.85, 0.80, 0.75, 0.70). The forecasts are generated using the first 12 months of demands, [x(1),…, x(12)]. The level, a, for the horizontal discount model is computed by,

$$a` = \sum xw / \sum w$$

where, $\sum xw = \sum x(\tau)w(t), \sum w = \sum w(t)$, and the history discount weights are $w(t) = \beta^{N-t}$.

The coefficients, a, b, for the trend discount model are obtained by the following:

$$b` = \left[\sum xw \sum tw - \sum w \sum xtw\right] / \left[\left(\sum tw\right)^2 - \sum w \sum t^2 w\right]$$

$$a` = \left[\sum xw - b \sum tw\right] / \sum w$$

where the summations range from t = 1 to 12. For brevity, the summation notations are: $\sum tw = \sum tw(t), \sum t^2 w = \sum t^2 w(t)$, and $\sum xtw = \sum x(t)tw(t)$

The cov of the forecast error is measured when the forecast is projected over the next 12 months of demand, [x(13),…, x(24)]. For simplicity, the cov for the horizontal forecast model is denoted as cov(H), and for the trend forecast model it is cov(T).

The samples are run 25 times and the average covs are listed in Table 8.3. Note from the table, the cov is best when the horizontal forecast model is applied, and also, the cov for the horizontal model gives more accurate results when the discount parameter, β, is near 0.95.

8.5 Cov by Parameter and Forecast Model when Trend Demands

This simulation is run to determine how the accuracy of the forecasts are affected for a trend demand pattern when the discount forecast models of horizontal and trend are in use and as the discount parameter varies. In this scenario, 24 months of demand history are randomly generated from a trend demand pattern where the monthly demands are slowly ramping upwards. Each demand is normally distributed with a mean $\mu(\tau) = (a + b\tau)$ and the standard deviation is $\sigma(\tau)$, where $\sigma(\tau) = cov \times \mu(\tau)$, and cov = 0.30. Because the mean of each month is slowly ramping up in this simulation, the associated standard deviation is also becoming larger with each month. The randomly generated demands are denoted as, x(1),…, x(24).

The forecasts are generated by the horizontal discount model and also by the trend discount model. The models use one parameter denoted as β. The values of β are: (0.95, 0.90, 0.85, 0.80, 0.75, 0.70). The forecasts are generated using the first 12 months of demands, [x(1),…, x(12)]. The level, a, for the horizontal discount model is computed by,

$$a` = \sum xw / \sum w$$

where, $\sum xw = \sum x(\tau)w(t)$, $\sum w = \sum w(t)$ and the history discount weights are $w(t) = \beta^{N-t}$.

The coefficients, a, b, for the trend discount model are obtained by the following:

$$b` = \left[\sum xw \sum tw - \sum w \sum xtw\right] / \left[\left(\sum tw\right)^2 - \sum w \sum t^2 w\right]$$

$$a` = \left[\sum xw - b \sum tw\right] / \sum w$$

Where the summations range from t = 1 to 12 and for notation brevity, $\sum tw = \sum tw(t)$, $\sum t^2 w = \sum t^2 w(t)$, and $\sum xtw = \sum x(t)tw(t)$.

The cov of the forecast error is measured when the forecast is projected over the next 12 months of demand, [x(13),…, x(24)]. For simplicity, the cov for the horizontal forecast model is denoted as cov(H), and for the trend forecast model it is cov(T).

The samples are run 25 times and the average covs are listed in Table 8.4. Note from the table results, the cov is best when the trend forecast model is applied, and also when the discount parameter, β, is near 0.95.

Table 8.4 Average cov from 25 samples by discount forecast model, horizontal and trend, and parameter β when true demand pattern is trend

β	Cov(H)	Cov(T)
0.95	0.676	0.341
0.90	0.646	0.344
0.85	0.619	0.350
0.80	0.596	0.362
0.75	0.576	0.386
0.70	0.560	0.438

8.6 Cov by Parameter and Forecast Model when Seasonal Demands

In this scenario, 36 months of demand history are randomly generated from a seasonal demand pattern where the monthly demands are slowly ramping upwards and have a seasonal cycle. This is the same seasonal data that is used in the Chap. 6 example. Each demand is normally distributed with a mean $\mu(\tau) = (a + bt)r(t)$ where a is the level, b is the slope and r(t) is the seasonal ratio for month t. The standard deviation is $\sigma(\tau)$, where $\sigma(\tau) = \text{cov} \times \mu(\tau)$, and cov = 0.30. Because the mean of each month is cycling up and down, the associated standard deviation is also changing with each month. The randomly generated demands are denoted as, x(1),…, x(36).

The seasonal smoothing multiplicative forecast model is used to generate the forecasts. The first 24 months of history demands are used to initialize the forecasts. The following three parameters, (α, β, γ), are needed where α is used to smooth the level, β is used to smooth the slope, and γ is used to smooth the seasonal ratios. The algorithm is the same as described in Chap. 6, and for brevity, it is not repeated here.

Since month t = 24 is the final history month, the forecasts for 12 subsequent months are projected in the following way:

$$f(\tau) = [a(24) + b(24)\,\tau]\,r(24 + \tau) \quad \tau = 1,\ldots,12$$

where the coefficients, a(24) and b(24), are the level and slope at month t = 24, and $r(24 + \tau)$ is the seasonal ratio for the τ-th future month. The cov for the model is based on the forecast error of the 12 future months, t = 25 to 36. Eight combinations of the three parameters are tried as listed in Table 8.6. For each combination, the cov is listed as cov(S). Note from the table, the best results are when the three parameters are set close to 0.10.

The trend smoothing forecast model is also applied with the same data, and uses only the parameter α and β. The cov is computed for future months t = 25 to 36 and the results, cov(T), are listed in Table 8.5 for four combination of parameter settings.

The horizontal smoothing forecast model is also applied with the same data and requires the parameter α. Two combinations of the parameter are tried and the cov is computed using the data of t = 25 to 36. The cov for these two combinations are listed in Table 8.5 under cov(H).

Table 8.5 Cov from seasonal smoothing forecast model, S, the trend smoothing forecast model, T, the horizontal smoothing model, H, and parameters α, β, γ, when true demand pattern is seasonal

α	β	γ	Cov(S)
0.10	0.10	0.10	0.332
0.10	0.10	0.20	0.342
0.10	0.20	0.10	0.335
0.20	0.10	0.10	0.351
0.10	0.20	0.20	0.346
0.20	0.10	0.20	0.365
0.20	0.20	0.10	0.398
0.20	0.20	0.20	0.417
α	*β*		*Cov(T)*
0.10	0.10		0.475
0.10	0.20		0.478
0.20	0.10		0.508
0.20	0.20		0.530
α			*Cov(H)*
0.10			0.558
0.20			0.563

Table 8.6 Twelve months of demand history, x(t), with one outlier demand and horizontal fit, f(t); and demand history with the outlier removed, x`(t), and resulting fit, f`(t)

Outlier			No outlier	
t	x(t)	f(t)	x`(t)	f`(t)
1	13	10.67	13	8.83
2	7	10.67	7	8.83
3	6	10.67	6	8.83
4	33	10.67	11	8.83
5	4	10.67	4	8.83
6	9	10.67	9	8.83
7	8	10.67	8	8.83
8	3	10.67	3	8.83
9	11	10.67	11	8.83
10	9	10.67	9	8.83
11	13	10.67	13	8.83
12	12	10.67	12	8.83

8.7 Cov when Horizontal Demands with an Outlier

The purpose of this simulation is to demonstrate how damaging an outlier demand is to the forecast results when an outlier is in the demand history. For this situation, $N=12$ months of demand history are randomly generated from a horizontal demand pattern where the individual monthly demands are normally distributed with a mean of μ and a standard deviation of $\sigma = \text{cov} \times \mu$ with $\text{cov} = 0.30$. The demands are

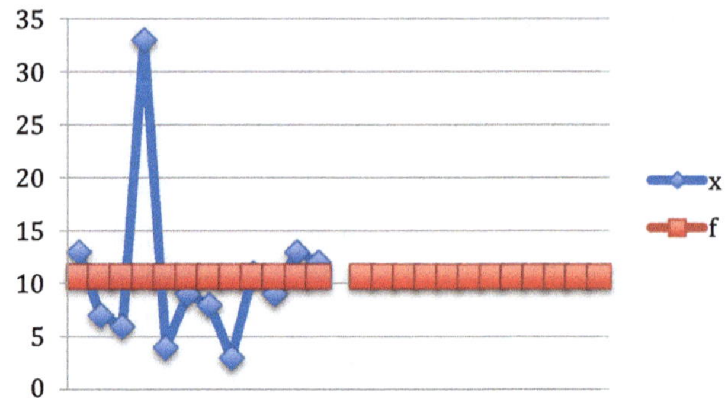

Fig. 8.1 Forecasts by horizontal model from horizontal demand pattern with one outlier

denoted as, x(1),…, x(N), where N=12. The demand in month t=4 is an outlier, with x(4)=33. The average demand is computed by,

$$a` = [x(1)+...+x(12)]/12$$

The residual errors of the history months is obtained, e(t)=(x(t)−a`) t=1 to 12, and the standard deviation estimate is computed as,

$$s = \sqrt{\sum e(t)^2/(12-1)}$$

So now, the coefficient of variation for this simulated sample is

$$cov = s/a`$$

Table 8.6 lists the 12 monthly demands, x(t) for t=1 to 12. The average demand is a` = 10.67 and the associated standard deviation is s=7.76. Thereby, the cov=7.76/10.67=0.727. These are the statistics when the outlier is not removed from the demand history. The table also lists the same demands when the outlier demand is removed, x`(t), and is adjusted to x`(4)=11, say. The average demand in this situation is a'=8.83 and the standard deviation is s=3.36, whereby, the cov is 3.36/8.83=0.380.

Figure 8.1 shows a plot of the demands with the outlier and the projected forecast for the next 12 months. Figure 8.2 depicts the same demands when the outlier is removed and adjusted, and projects the forecast for 12 future months.

Should the outlier not be adjusted, the forecast would call for f =10.67 pieces per month, and in inventory control, the related standard deviation would be s=7.76 causing a need for much safety stock. Without the outlier, the forecast would be f=8.83 pieces per month and the standard deviation would be 3.36. The results show how outliers cause a large and unnecessary increase in the inventory needs. Chapter 9 describes a way to detect and modify outliers in the demand history.

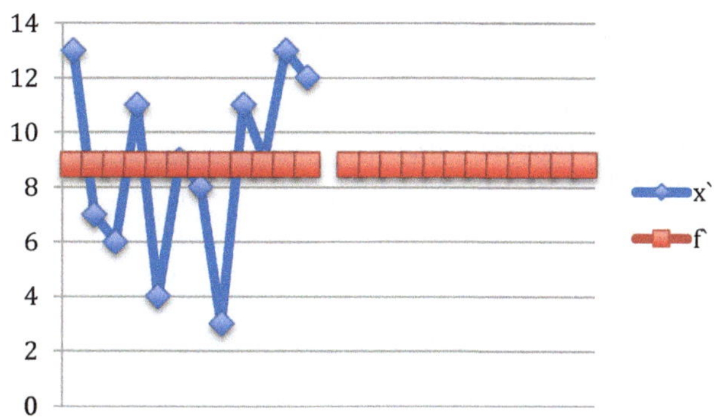

Fig. 8.2 Forecasts by horizontal regression model from horizontal demand pattern with the outlier adjusted

8.8 Cov when Trend Demands with an Outlier

The purpose of this simulation is to demonstrate how damaging an undetected outlier in the demand history is to the forecasts when the demand pattern is a trend. In this situation, 24 months of demand history is randomly generated from a trend demand pattern where the monthly demands are slowly ramping upwards. Each demand is normally distributed with a mean $\mu(\tau) = (a + b\tau)$ and the standard deviation is $\sigma(\tau)$, where $\sigma(\tau) = \text{cov} \times \mu(t)$, and cov=0.30. Because the mean of each month is slowly ramping up in this simulation, the associated standard deviation is also becoming larger with each month. The randomly generated demands are denoted as, x(1),…, x(24).

Assume N=12 history months, [x(1),…, X(12)], are available to generate the forecasts, and the next 12 demands, [X(13),…, X(24)], are used to estimate the accuracy of the forecast. The fit of the demands has two coefficients, (a, b), and these are estimated as follows:

$$b` = \left[\sum x \sum t - N \sum xt\right] / \left[\left(\sum t\right)^2 - N \sum t^2\right]$$

$$a` = \left[\sum x - b \sum t\right] / N$$

Where the summations range from t=1 to 12 and for brevity, the summations are: $\sum x = \sum x(t)$ and $\sum xt = \sum x(t)t$.

The fitted values for the history months are computed by,

$$f(t) = a` + b`\,t \quad t = 1 \text{ to } N$$

The level at t=N becomes:

$$a(12) = (a` + 12b`)$$

Table 8.7 Twelve months of demand history, x(t), with one outlier demand and trend fit, f(t), and demand history with outlier removed, x`(t), and resulting fit, f`(t)

Outlier			No outlier	
t	x(t)	f(t)	x(t)`	f(t)`
1	27	18.55	27	16.05
2	15	19.03	15	16.39
3	12	19.50	12	16.73
4	22	19.98	22	17.07
5	9	20.45	9	17.41
6	17	20.93	17	17.75
7	56	21.40	17	18.09
8	6	21.88	6	18.43
9	22	22.36	22	18.76
10	18	22.83	18	19.10
11	27	23.31	27	19.44
12	23	23.78	23	19.78

and so, the forecasts for the τ-th future month is,

$$f(\tau) = a(12) + b`\tau \qquad \tau = 1 \text{ to } 12$$

The forecast error is measured for each of the future 12 months by,

$$e(\tau) = (x(\tau) - f(\tau)) \qquad \tau = 1 \text{ to } 12$$

and the standard deviation is measured as follows,

$$s = \sqrt{\sum e(t)^2 / (12-1)}$$

Because the projected average forecast for the future 12 months, t=13 to 24, is [a(12)+6.5b`], the coefficient of variation is measured as below:

$$cov = s / [a(12){+}6.5b`]$$

The 12 history demands, [x(1),…, x(12)], that includes an outlier, are listed in the 2nd column of Table 8.7 as x(t), and their associated fitted values, f(t), are in the 3rd column. The outlier is in month t=7 where x(7)=56. The level and slope at t=12 become: a`(12)=23.78 and b`=0.47. The forecasts for the future 12 months are generated and the coefficient of variation becomes, cov=0.501.

When the outlier is removed and adjusted to x(7)=17, say, the estimates of the level and slope at t=12 become: a`(12)=19.78 and b`=0.34. The forecasts are projected for the 12 future months and the coefficient of variation becomes, cov=0.316.

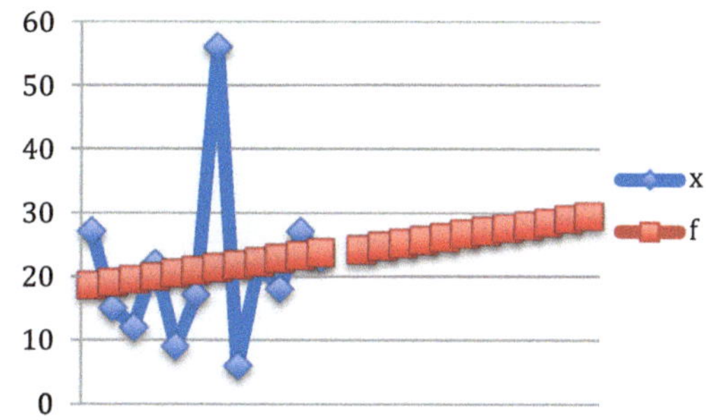

Fig. 8.3 Forecasts by trend regression model from trend demand pattern with an outlier

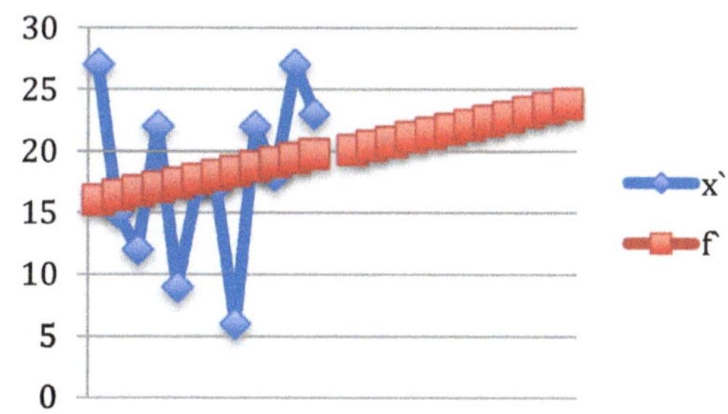

Fig. 8.4 Forecasts by trend regression model from trend demand pattern with the outlier adjusted

Figure 8.3 is a plot of the demands with the outlier and the projected forecast for the next 12 months. Figure 8.4 depicts the same demands when the outlier is removed and adjusted prior to forecasting, and projects the forecast for 12 future months.

Summary

The more accurate the forecasts, the better the inventory decisions on when and how much stock to carry for each item in a stocking location. These decisions are vital to the profitability of the entity at all of its inventory locations. The coefficient of variation of the 1 month ahead forecast error is used to measure the forecast accuracy. A series of simulations are run to determine how the number of months of demand history affects the cov when the demand history is from a horizontal demand pattern and from a trend demand pattern. Another series of simulations are aimed at measuring the forecast accuracy depending on the parameters and the forecast model chosen for an item when the demand pattern is horizontal, trend or seasonal. Another series of simulations are run to measure how an outlier demand in the demand history influences the accuracy of the forecast.

Chapter 9
Filtering Outliers

9.1 Introduction

A primary goal of forecasting is to measure the flow of demands from the history months and project to the future months with a minimum forecast error. A way to enhance this goal is by filtering the history demands to seek out any outlier demands and adjust accordingly. As demonstrated in the prior chapter, outlier demands cause much damage to the forecasts and increase the forecast error. Filtering of the demand history is not an easy process, but is important to yield forecasts with minimal forecast error. Reducing the forecast error will reduce the amount of safety stock needed to run the inventory operation. This chapter shows a way to seek out and adjust any outlier demands from the history months when the demand patterns are of the horizontal, trend or seasonal type. The filtering process takes place just prior to generating the forecasts.

Another way to minimize outlier demands is by filtering the line demands that occur in the order entry phase of the inventory stocking location. This is when the customers send in the purchase orders and list on each line of the order, a part number and a quantity. This part number request is a line demand and can be filtered to seek if it an outlier. If an outlier is detected here, the line demand is sent back to the customer seeking verification on the quantity.

9.2 Horizontal Filtering

Suppose the horizontal demand pattern where N history demand entries, x(1),…, x(N), are to be used to generate a horizontal forecast. Prior to forecasting, the demands are filtered seeking if any outlier demands, and if so, the outlier is adjusted accordingly. A way to do this is described in the following seven steps.

N. T. Thomopoulos, *Demand Forecasting for Inventory Control*,
DOI 10.1007/978-3-319-11976-2_9

9.2.1 *Horizontal Filtering Algorithm (HFA)*

1. For each x(t), find the absolute average difference, called the difference measure and denoted as d(t), from its closest neighbors as follows:

$$d(t) = |x(t) - 0.5[x(t-1) + x(t+1)]| \quad \text{for} \quad t = 2 \text{ to } N-1$$

$$d(1) = |x(1) - x(2)| \quad \text{for} \quad t = 1$$

$$d(N) = |x(N) - x(N-1)| \quad \text{for} \quad t = N$$

2. Locate the maximum d(t), denoted as dmx, and call the month tmx where the associated demand is x(tmx).
3. For month tmx, get the adjusted demand as the average of its closest neighbors as below:

$$x`(tmx) = [x(tmx-1) + x(tmx+1)]/2 \quad \text{if } tmx = 2 \text{ to } N-1$$

$$x`(tmx) = x(2) \quad \text{if } tmx = 1$$

$$x`(tmx) = x(N-1) \quad \text{if } tmx = N$$

Let x`(t) = x(t) for all months other than t = tmx.

4. Using the N demands, x`(t), compute the fitted value f(t) using the horizontal model. For the horizontal forecast model, the fitted values for each history month is $f(t) = \bar{x}$, the average value.
5. Compute the residual errors, e(t) = x`(t)-f(t), for all months t = 1 to N.
6. Using the N residual errors, calculate the standard deviation estimate as,

$$s = \sqrt{\sum e(t)^2/(N-1)}$$

7. Now compute a t-ratio as,

$$T = [x(tmx) - f(tmx)]/s$$

8. Choose a limit U, say U = 3, to be compared to the absolute value of T to determine if the demand, x(tmx) is an outlier.
   If $|T| > U$, then x(tmx) is an outlier.
9. If x(tmx) is an outlier, repeat the steps, (1–8) for a limited number of cycles, Nc, per part number, perhaps two cycles. If x(tmx) is not an outlier, use the original series, x(t) t = 1 to N, to generate the forecasts; else, use the adjusted series, x` (t) t = 1 to N.

Example 9.1 Consider the *N* = 12 demand entries, as shown in Table 9.1 where the horizontal forecast model is to be applied. Assume the filtering parameters are U = 3 and Nc = 1. This is an example where the history demands have no outliers. Below is a summary of the filtering algorithm for this example:

Table 9.1 Horizontal filtering worksheet, history months, t, demand history, x(t), difference measures, d(t), adjusted demands, x`(t), and fitted demands, f(t)

t	x(t)	d(t)	x`(t)	f(t)
1	29	20	29	16.33
2	9	8	9	16.33
3	5	11	5	16.33
4	23	6	23	16.33
5	29	17	29	16.33
6	1	26	27	16.33
7	25	23	25	16.33
8	3	16	3	16.33
9	13	6.5	13	16.33
10	10	1	10	16.33
11	5	9	5	16.33
12	18	13	18	16.33

1. Get d(t) t = 1 to 12
2. dmx = max[d(t)] = 26
   tmx = 6
   x(6) = 1
3. x`(t) = x(t) t = 1 to 12, but not for t = 6
   x`(6) = 0.5[x(5) + x(7)] = 0.5(29 + 25) = 27
4. $\bar{x}$ = 16.33
   f(t) = 16.33 t = 1 to 12
5. Get e(t) = [x`(t) – f(t)] t = 1 to 12
6. s = 10.47
7. T = [x(6) - f(6)]/s = [1 – 16.33]/10.47 = -1.47
8. Since |T| < U = 3, x(6) = 1 is not an outlier.
9. Use x(t) t = 1 to 12 in forecasting.

Example 9.2 Consider the $N=12$ demand entries, as shown in Table 9.2 where the horizontal forecast model is to be applied. The filtering parameters are U=3 and Nc=1. This also is an example where the filtering process finds no outliers. Below is a summary of the filtering algorithm for this example:

1. Get d(t) t = 1 to 12
2. dmx = max[d(t)] = 24
   tmx = 1
   x(1) = 24
3. x`(t) = x(t) t = 1 to 12, but not t = 1
   x`(1) = x(2) = 0
4. $\bar{x}$ = 4.17
   f(t) = 4.17 t = 1 to 12
5. Get e(t) = [x`(t) – f(t)] t = 1 to 12
6. s = 8.03
7. T = [x(1) - f(1)]/s = [24 – 4.17]/8.03 = 2.47
8. Since |T| < U = 3, x(1) = 24 is not an outlier.
9. Use x(t) t = 1 to 12 in forecasting.

Table 9.2 Horizontal filtering worksheet, history months, t, demand history, x(t), difference measure, d(t), adjusted demands, x`(t), fitted demands, f(t)

t	x(t)	d(t)	x`(t)	f(t)
1	24	24	0	4.17
2	0	12	0	4.17
3	0	6	0	4.17
4	12	1	12	4.17
5	22	16	22	4.17
6	0	18.5	0	4.17
7	15	15	15	4.17
8	0	7.5	0	4.17
9	0	0	0	4.17
10	0	0	0	4.17
11	0	0.5	0	4.17
12	1	1	1	4.17

Example 9.3 Consider the $N=12$ demand entries, as shown in Table 9.3 where the horizontal forecast model is applied. The filtering parameters are the following: upper limit on T is U=3.0 and number of filter cycles is Nc=1. In this example, the filtering process finds one outlier at t=5. Below is a summary of the filtering algorithm for this example:

1. Get d(t)   t = 1 to 12
2. dmx = max[d(t)] = 51.5
   tmx = 5
   x(5) = 55
3. x`(t) = x(t)   t = 1 to 12, but not for t = 5
   x`(5) = [x(4) + x(6)]/2 = 3.5
4. $\bar{x}$ = 3.71
   f(t) = 3.71   t = 1 to 12
5. Get e(t) = [x`(t) – f(t)]   t = 1 to 12
6. s = 2.01
7. T = [x(5) - f(5)]/s = [55 – 3.71]/2.01 = 25.57
8. Since |T| > U = 3, x(5) = 55 is an outlier.
9. Because Nc = 1, the filtering process ends and use x`(t) in forecasting.

Example 9.4 Consider the $N=24$ demand entries, as shown in Table 9.4 where the horizontal forecast model is to be applied. The filtering parameters are the following: upper limit on T is U=3.0 and number of filter cycles is Nc=2. Below is a summary of the filtering algorithm for this example. For this part's demand history, two outliers are detected. Table 9.4 is a worksheet for the first filtering cycle and Table 9.5 is the worksheet for second filtering cycle.

Table 9.3 Horizontal filtering worksheet, history months, t, demand history, x(t), difference measure, d(t), adjusted demands, x`(t), fitted demands, f(t)

t	x(t)	d(t)	x`(t)	f(t)
1	7	4	7	3.71
2	3	1.5	3	3.71
3	2	2.5	2	3.71
4	6	22.5	6	3.71
5	55	51.5	3.5	3.71
6	1	29.5	1	3.71
7	6	4.5	6	3.71
8	2	3	2	3.71
9	4	1.5	4	3.71
10	3	0	3	3.71
11	2	2	2	3.71
12	5	3	5	3.71

Table 9.4 Horizontal filtering worksheet of cycle 1 for Example 9.4, history months, t, demand history, x(t), difference measure, d(t), adjusted demands, x`(t), fitted demands, f(t)

t	x(t)	d(t)	x`(t)	f(t)
1	17	10	17	13.71
2	7	4	7	13.71
3	5	5.5	5	13.71
4	14	3.5	14	13.71
5	16	31	16	13.71
6	80	65	80	13.71
7	14	28	14	13.71
8	4	7.5	4	13.71
9	9	3.5	9	13.71
10	7	0	7	13.71
11	5	4	5	13.71
12	11	4	11	13.71
13	9	6.5	9	13.71
14	20	10	20	13.71
15	11	4.5	11	13.71
16	11	46.5	11	13.71
17	104	96	8.0	13.71
18	5	54	5	13.71
19	14	6	14	13.71
20	11	0.5	11	13.71
21	9	4.5	9	13.71
22	16	4.5	16	13.71
23	14	0	14	13.71
24	12	2	12	13.71

Table 9.5 Horizontal filtering worksheet of cycle 2 for Example 9.4, history months, t, demand history, x(t), difference measure, d(t), adjusted demands, x`(t), fitted demands, f(t)

t	x(t)	d(t)	x`(t)	f(t)
1	17	10	17	11.00
2	7	4	7	11.00
3	5	5.5	5	11.00
4	14	3.5	14	11.00
5	16	31	16	11.00
6	80	65	15.0	11.00
7	14	28	14	11.00
8	4	7.5	4	11.00
9	9	3.5	9	11.00
10	7	0	7	11.00
11	5	4	5	11.00
12	11	4	11	11.00
13	9	6.5	9	11.00
14	20	10	20	11.00
15	11	4.5	11	11.00
16	11	1.5	11	11.00
17	8	0	8	11.00
18	5	6	5	11.00
19	14	6	14	11.00
20	11	0.5	11	11.00
21	9	4.5	9	11.00
22	16	4.5	16	11.00
23	14	0	14	11.00
24	12	2	12	11.00

The nine filter steps of cycle 1 of Example 9.4 are below. The worksheet is Table 9.4.

1. Get d(t) t = 1 to 24
2. dmx = max[d(t)] = 96
   tmx = 17
   x(17) = 104
3. x`(t) = x(t) t = 1 to 24, but not t = 17
   x`(17) = [x(16) + x(18)]/2 = 8.0
4. $\bar{x}$ = 13.71
   f(t) = 13.71 t = 1 to 24
5. Get e(t) = [x`(t) – f(t)] t = 1 to 24
6. s = 15.07
7. T = [x(17) - f(17)]/s = [104 – 13.71]/15.07 = 5.99
8. Since |T| > U = 3, x(17) = 104 is an outlier.
9. Because Nc = 2, perform another filter cycle.

Below is a summary of the filtering cycle 2 for the part in Example 9.4. Note Table 9.5 where an outlier is detected in history month t=6.

The filter steps of cycle 2 of Example 9.4 are below. The worksheet is Table 9.5.

1. Set x(t) = x`(t) from filter cycle 1 and get d(t) t = 1 to 24
2. dmx = max[d(t)] = 65
   tmx = 6
   x(6) = 80
3. x`(t) = x(t) t = 1 to 24, but not for t = 6
   x`(6) = [x(5) + x(7)]/2 = 15.0
4. $\bar{x}$ = 11.00
   f(t) = 11.00 t = 1 to 24
5. Get e(t) = [x`(t) – f(t)] t = 1 to 24
6. s = 4.42
7. T = [x(6) - f(6)]/s = [80 – 11.0]/4.42 = 15.60
8. Since |T| > U = 3, x(6) = 80 is an outlier.
9. Because Nc = 2, stop filtering and use x`(t) in forecasting.

9.3 Trend Filtering

When the trend forecast model is to be applied for a part, the trend filtering algorithm (TFA) is applied to the demand history seeking and adjusting any outliers. The only difference between TFA and HFA is the method of generating the fitted values for the history months. The fitted values for HFA is simply the average value of the adjusted demand history, and for TFA, the fitted values is a trend flow over the history months. The trend filter algorithm is summarized below.

9.3.1 Trend Filtering Algorithm (TFA)

1. For each x(t), find the absolute average difference, called the difference measure and denoted as d(t), from its closest neighbors as follows:

$$d(t) = |x(t) - 0.5[x(t-1) + x(t+1)]| \quad \text{for } t = 2 \text{ to } N-1$$

$$d(1) = |x(1) - x(2)| \quad \text{for } t = 1$$

$$d(N) = |x(N) - x(N-1)| \quad \text{for } t = N$$

2. Locate the maximum d(t), denoted as dmx, and call the month tmx where the associated demand is x(tmx).

3. For month tmx, get the adjusted demand from the average of its closest neighbors as below:

$$x`(tmx) = [x(tmx-1) + x(tmx+1)]/2 \quad \text{if } tmx = 2 \text{ to } N-1$$

$$x`(tmx) = x(2) \quad \text{if } tmx = 1$$

$$x`(tmx) = x(N-1) \quad \text{if } tmx = N$$

Let $x`(t) = x(t)$ for all months other than $t = tmx$.

4. For the N demands, x`(t), compute the fitted value f(t) using the trend forecast model. For the trend forecast model, the fitted values for each history month is f(t) = (a` + b`t), where a` and b` are estimates of the level and slope, respectively. One way to compute the level and slope is by way of the trend regression model as follows:

$$b` = \left[\sum x \sum t - N \sum xt\right] / \left[\left(\sum t\right)^2 - N \sum t^2\right]$$

$$a` = \left[\sum x - b \sum t\right] / N$$

where $\sum x = \sum x(t)$ and $\sum xt = \sum x(t)t$ and all the sums are for t = 1 to N.

5. Compute the residual errors, e(t) = x`(t) − f(t), for all months t = 1 to N.
6. Using the N residual errors, calculate the standard deviation estimate as,

$$s = \sqrt{\sum e(t)^2 / (N-2)}$$

7. Now compute t-ratio as,

$$T = [x(tmx) - f(tmx)]/s$$

8. Choose a limit U, say U = 3, to be compared to T to determine if the demand, x(tmx) is an outlier.

If $|T| > U$, x(tmx) is an outlier.

9. If x(tmx) is an outlier, repeat the steps, (1–8) for a limited number of cycles, Nc, per part number, perhaps two cycles. If x(tmx) is not an outlier, use the original series, x(t) t = 1 to N to generate the forecasts; else, use the adjusted series, x`(t) t = 1 to N.

Example 9.5 Consider the $N = 24$ demand entries, as shown in Table 9.6 where the trend forecast model is under review. The filtering parameters are the following: upper limit on T is U = 3.0, and number of filter cycles is Nc = 1. Below is a summary of the filtering algorithm for this example. For this part's demand history, no outlier is detected. The table is a worksheet for the filtering cycle.

Table 9.6 Trend filtering worksheet for Example 9.5, history months, t, demand history, x(t), difference measure, d(t), adjusted demands, x`(t), fitted demands, f(t)

t	x(t)	d(t)	x`(t)	f(t)
1	14	8.00	14	8.47
2	6	3.50	6	9.06
3	5	5.00	5	9.66
4	14	3.00	14	10.25
5	17	8.50	17	10.84
6	3	13.50	16.5	11.42
7	16	12.50	16	12.02
8	4	9.50	4	12.61
9	11	4.50	11	13.20
10	9	0.50	9	13.79
11	6	6.00	6	14.38
12	15	6.00	15	14.98
13	12	9.50	12	15.57
14	28	13.50	28	16.16
15	17	5.00	17	16.75
16	16	2.00	16	17.34
17	19	7.00	19	17.93
18	8	12.50	8	18.52
19	22	8.50	22	19.11
20	19	0.00	19	19.70
21	16	8.00	16	20.30
22	29	8.50	29	20.89
23	25	0.50	25	21.48
24	22	3.00	22	22.07

The filter steps of Example 9.5 are listed below. The worksheet is Table 9.6

1. Get d(t) t = 1 to 24
2. dmx = max[d(t)] = 13.5
   tmx = 6
   x(6) = 3
3. x`(t) = x(t) t = 1 to 24, but not for t = 6
   x`(6) = [x(5) + x(7)]/2 = 16.5
4. a` = 7.88
   b` = 0.59
   f(t) = 7.88 + 0.59t for t = 1 to 24
   f(6) = 11.42
5. Get e(t) = [x`(t) – f(t)] t = 1 to 24
6. s = 5.64
7. T = [x(6) - f(6)]/s = [3 – 11.42]/5.64 = 1.49
8. Since |T| < U = 3, x(6) = 3 is not an outlier.
9. Use x(t) in forecasting.

Table 9.7 Trend filtering worksheet for Example 9.6, history months, t, demand history, x(t), difference measure, d(t), adjusted demands, x`(t), fitted demands, f(t)

t	x(t)	d(t)	x`(t)	f(t)
1	14	8	14	11.42
2	6	3.5	6	11.36
3	5	5	5	11.31
4	14	3	14	11.26
5	17	29	17	11.20
6	78	61.5	16.5	11.15
7	16	25	16	11.09
8	4	9.5	4	11.04
9	11	4.5	11	10.98
10	9	0.5	9	10.93
11	6	6	6	10.88
12	15	9	15	10.82

Example 9.6 Consider the $N = 12$ demand entries, as shown in Table 9.7 where the trend forecast model is under review. The filtering parameters are the following: upper limit on T is U = 3.0 and number of filter cycles is Nc = 1. Below is a summary of the filtering algorithm for this example. For this part's demand history, an outlier is detected. The table is a worksheet for the filtering cycle.
Filter cycle 1 of Example 9.5:

1. Get d(t) t = 1 to 12
2. dmx = max[d(t)] = 61.5
   tmx = 6
   x(6) = 78
3. x`(t) = x(t) t = 1 to 12, but not for t = 6
   x`(6) = [x(5) + x(7)]/2 = 16.5
4. a` = 11.48
   b` = -0.06
   f(t) = (11.48 - 0.06×t) for t = 1 to 12
   f(6) = 11.15
5. Get e(t) = [x`(t) – f(t)] t = 1 to 12
6. s = 5.13
7. T = [x(6) - f(6)]/s = [78 – 11.15]/5.13 = 13.02
8. Since |T| > U = 3, x(6) = 78 is an outlier.
9. Because Nc = 1, stop filtering and use x'(t) in forecasting.

9.4 Seasonal Filtering

When the seasonal multiplicative forecast model is to be applied for a part, the seasonal filtering algorithm (SFA) is run to the demand history for which it is seeking and adjusting any outliers. The only difference between SFA and the prior filtering algorithms (TFA, HFA) is the method of generating the fitted values for the history months. The fitted value for HFA is the average value of the adjusted demand history, and for TFA, the fitted value is the trend flow over the history months. For SFA, the fitted values require a seasonal flow where the coefficients for the level, a`, slope, b`, and 12 seasonal ratios, r(j) j = 1 to 12, are needed. For a review, the seasonal filter algorithm is summarized below.

9.4.1 Seasonal Filtering Algorithm (SFA)

1. For each x(t), find the absolute average difference, called the difference measure and denoted as d(t), from its closest neighbors as follows:

$$d(t) = |x(t) - 0.5[x(t-1) + x(t+1)]| \quad \text{for } t = 2 \text{ to } N-1$$

$$d(1) = |x(1) - x(2)| \quad \text{for } t = 1$$

$$d(N) = |x(N) - x(N-1)| \quad \text{for } t = N$$

2. Locate the maximum d(t), denoted as dmx, and call the month tmx where the associated demand is x(tmx).
3. For month tmx, get the adjusted demand as the average of its closest neighbors as below:

$$x`(tmx) = [x(tmx-1) + x(tmx+1)]/2 \quad \text{if } tmx = 2 \text{ to } N-1$$

$$x`(tmx) = x(2) \quad \text{if } tmx = 1$$

$$x`(tms) = x(N-1) \quad \text{if } tmx = N$$

Let x`(t) = x(t) for all months other than t = tmx.

4. For the N demands, x`(t), compute the fitted value f(t). For the seasonal forecast model, the fitted values for each history month is f(t) = (a` + b`t)r(t), where a` and b` are estimates of the level and slope, respectively, and r(t) is the seasonal ratio for month t. A way to compute the level and slope is by way of the seasonal model described in Chapter 5. A quick review is below:

At the start, the seasonal smoothing parameters (α, β, γ) are selected for the model. The nine stages to initialize the seasonal forecast model are listed below when the months of history is $N=24$:

1. X1 = [x(1) + ... + x(12)]/12
2. X2 = [x(13) + ... + x(24)]/12
3. b`(0) = [X2 – X1]/12
4. a`(0) = X1 – 6.5b(0)
5. a`(t) = a`(0)+ b`(0)t   t = 1 to 24
6. r`(t) = x(t)/a`(t)   t = 1 to 24
7. r(t) = [r`(t) + r`(t+12]/2   t = 1 to 12
8. a(0) = a`(0) and b(0) = b`(0)
9. Do the following for t = 1 to 24
   a(t) = α [x(t)/r(t)] + (1-α)[a(t-1)+b(t-1)]
   b(t) = β [a(t) – a(t-1)] + (1-β)[b(t-1)]
   r(t+12) = γ [x(t)/a(t)] + (1-γ)[r(t)]
   f(t) = a(t)r(12+t)

In this example,

5. Compute the residual errors, e(t) = [x(t) − f(t)], for all months t = 1 to N.
6. The standard deviation estimate is revised each history month, t, as follows:

$$\mathrm{s}(t)=\sqrt{\alpha e(t)^2+(1-\alpha)s(t-1)^2}$$

7. The final standard deviation, s(N), is used to compute T-ratio as below:

$$\mathrm{T}=[\mathrm{x(tmx)}-\mathrm{f(tmx)}]/\mathrm{s\ (N)}$$

8. Choose a limit U, say U = 3, to be compared to T to determine if the demand, x(tmx) is an outlier.
   If $|\mathrm{T}| > \mathrm{U}, \mathrm{x(tmx)}$ is an outlier.
9. If x(tmx) is an outlier, repeat the steps, (1–8) for a limited number of cycles, Nc, per part number, perhaps two cycles. If x(tmx) is not an outlier, use the original series, x(t) t = 1 to N to generate the forecasts; else, use the adjusted series, x`(t) t = 1 to N.

Example 9.7 Consider the $N=24$ demand entries, as shown in Table 9.8 where the seasonal forecast model is under review. The filtering parameters are the following: upper limit on T is U = 3.0, and number of filter cycles is Nc = 1. Below is a summary of the filtering algorithm for this example. For this part's demand history, an outlier is detected. The table is a worksheet for the filtering cycle.

Table 9.8 Seasonal filtering worksheet for Example 9.7, history months, t, demand history, x(t), difference measure, d(t), adjusted demands, x`(t), fitted demands, f(t)

t	x(t)	d(t)	x`(t)	f(t)
1	15	4	15	8.99
2	11	2	11	13.41
3	11	7.5	11	12.03
4	26	2.5	26	19.03
5	36	15.5	36	26.42
6	15	20.5	15	14.05
7	35	21	35	28.74
8	13	14	13	17.17
9	19	37.5	19	16.87
10	100	86	14.0	17.10
11	9	47	9	12.60
12	12	1.5	12	11.14
13	12	10	12	17.69
14	32	13	32	25.41
15	26	4	26	22.06
16	28	3.5	28	33.85
17	37	11	37	45.75
18	24	15.5	24	23.73
19	42	13	42	47.49
20	34	0.5	34	27.78
21	25	7.5	25	26.79
22	31	6.5	31	26.69
23	24	0.5	24	19.36
24	16	8	16	16.85

Filter cycle 1 of Example 9.7:

1. Get d(t) t = 1 to 24
2. dmx = max[d(t)] = 86
   tmx = 10
   x(10) = 100
3. x`(t) = x(t) t = 1 to 24, but not for t = 10
   x`(10) = [x(9) + x(11)]/2 = 14.0
4. Run the initial stage of the seasonal forecast model for t = 1 to 24. The fit at t = 10 is f(10) = 17.10.
5. Get e(t) = [x`(t) – f(t)] t = 1 to 24
6. s = s(24) = 5.15
7. T = [x(10) - f(10)]/s = [100 – 17.10]/5.15 = 16.10
8. Since |T| > U = 3, x(10) = 100 is an outlier.
9. Because Nc = 1, stop filtering and use x`(t) in forecasting.

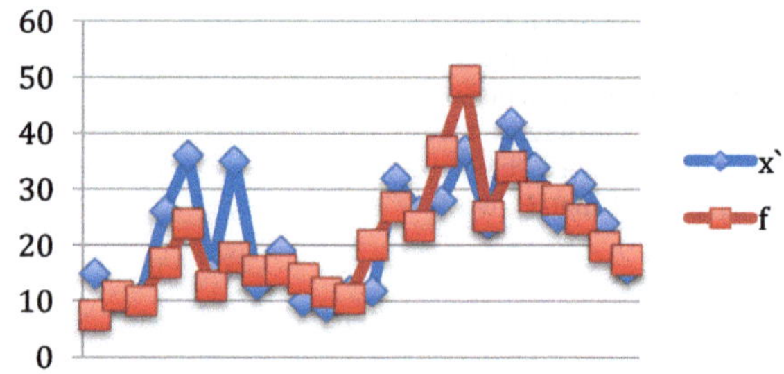

Fig. 9.1 Example 9.7 filtered demand history, x`(t), and fit, f(t), for seasonal model

Figure 9.1 is a depiction of the data from Example 9.7 with $N=24$ months of demand history. The plot compares the adjusted demand entries, x(t), and the fitted demands, f(t), for each history month.

9.5 Filtering Line Demands in Order Entry

Another way to prevent outliers from occurring in the demand history is to filter the line demands at the order entry level stage early on, when the customers send in their orders. In order entry, the customer order is received with one or more line items. Each line is for a different part, and the line identifies the part and the quantity of the purchase. The quantity is here called the line demand and labeled as d. For month t, the number of lines for a part is denoted as n(t), and the total demands for the part is x(t). The i-th demand for the part in month t is denoted as $d_{(i,t)}$. For month t,

$$x(t) = \sum_{i=1}^{n(t)} d_{(i,t)}$$

It is impractical for most companies to save history on all the line demands, $d_{(i,t)}$, for each part in the inventory. Instead, most companies may save the history of monthly number of lines, n(t), and the corresponding monthly demands, x(t), for the prior N months of history.

With this history, it is possible to compute the average and standard deviation of the line demand, d. These are labeled as $\bar{d}$ for the average and s_d for the standard deviation. With these, the management can select a safety factor, k, (typically k=3 or 4), and compute lower and upper limits for each part number as follows:

$$LL = \bar{d} - ks_d$$

$$UL = \bar{d} + ks_d$$

The limits are then used in the order entry system to filter each incoming line demand, d, of the part in the following way:

If $LL \le d \le UL$ accept d

Table 9.9 Demand history for $N=12$ months, where t=history months, n(t)=number lines in t, x(t)=demand in t, and $d_{(i,\ t)}$=individual line demands in t

t	n(t)	x(t)	$d_{(i,\ t)}$				
1	4	6	2	2	1	1	
2	4	7	1	2	2	2	
3	0	0					
4	2	5	3	2			
5	2	6	3	3			
6	0	0					
7	5	8	1	2	2	1	2
8	2	3	1	2			
9	3	4	1	1	2		
10	4	9	2	3	3	1	
11	3	6	3	1	2		
12	1	3	3				

if $d < LL$ verify d

if $d > UL$ verify d

Oftentimes, the lower limit is negative, whereby, only the line demands greater than the upper limit are filtered.

For notational convenience in the following developments, the number of lines over the N months of demand history is labeled as L where:

$$L = \sum_{t=1}^{N} n(t)$$

The average and standard deviation of the line demands are computed as below:

$$\bar{d} = \sum_{t=1}^{N} x(t) \Big/ \sum_{t=1}^{N} n(t)$$

$$s = \left\{ \sum_{t=1}^{N} \left[x(t) - n(t)\bar{d} \right]^2 L \Big/ \left[L^2 - \sum_{t=1}^{N} n(t)^2 \right] \right\}^{0.5}$$

The mathematical verification of this result is provided subsequently in this chapter.

Example 9.8 Consider a part with $N=12$ months of demand history as shown in Table 9.9. The table lists the months of history, t, the number of lines in the month, n(t), the demand in the month, x(t), and the individual line demands per month as $d_{(i,\ t)}$ for i=1 to n(t). The management wants to establish lower and upper limits on future incoming line demands, d. For this example, assume the safety factor is set to k=3.0. The computations are below where the summations range from t=1 to N.

$$\sum n(t) = 30$$

$$\sum x(t) = 57$$

$$\sum n(t)^2 = 104$$

$$\bar{d} = \sum x(t) / \sum n(t) = 1.90$$

$$S_d = \left\{ \sum \left[x(t) - n(t)\bar{d} \right]^2 L / \left[L^2 - \sum n(t)^2 \right] \right\}^{0.5} = 0.83$$

$$LL = \bar{d} - ks_d = -0.59$$

$$UL = \bar{d} + ks_d = 4.39$$

Since the lower limit, LL, is negative, the lower limit is reset to LL=0. Also, because, the upper limit is not an integer, it is set to the next higher integer, UL=5. So, the order entry system for this part would filter each line demand, d, in the following way:

If $d \le 5$, the line demand is accepted.
If $d > 5$, the line is returned to the customer for verification.

9.6 Derivation of Mean and Standard Deviation of Line Demands

In the following verification, the notation for the true mean and variance of the line demand, d, are denoted as μ and σ^2, respectively. The corresponding estimates are labeled as: $\bar{d}$ and s_d^2. The goal here is to find unbiased estimates of the true mean and variance using only the demand history data listed below:

x(t)=demands in month t for t=1 to N
n(t)=number of lines in month t for t=1 to N

For each month t, the demands consist of the sum of all line demands in the month as follows:

$$x(t) = \left[d_{(1,t)} + \ldots + d_{(n(t),t)} \right] \quad \text{for } t = 1 \text{ to } N$$

The line demands, $d_{(i,\ t)}$ are not known and only the quantities, n(t) and x(t) are known.

The average of the line demands is computed as follows:

$$\bar{d} = \sum_{t=1}^{N} x(t) \Big/ \sum_{t=1}^{N} n(t)$$

The expected value of $\bar{d}$ is obtained below.

$$E(\bar{d}) = E\left[\sum_{t=1}^{N} x(t) \Big/ \sum_{t=1}^{N} n(t)\right] = \sum_{t=1}^{N} n(t)\mu \Big/ \sum_{t=1}^{N} n(t) = \mu$$

Thereby, the average, $\bar{d}$, is an unbiased estimator of the true mean, μ.

For notational ease, let L represent the total number of lines in the N months of history, whereby,

$$L = \sum_{t=1}^{N} n(t)$$

Note, the expected value of x(t) is below.

$$E[x(t)] = n(t)\mu,$$

The square of the residual error, $[x(t) - n(t)\bar{d}]^2$, is listed below.

$$[x(t) - n(t)\bar{d}]^2 = [x(t)^2] + [(n(t)\bar{d})^2] - 2[x(t)n(t)\bar{d}]$$

From the above expression, the expected values of the three components on the right-hand-side are listed below.

$$E[x(t)^2] = n(t)[n(t)\mu^2 + \sigma^2]$$

$$E[(n(t)\bar{d})^2] = n(t)^2[\mu^2 + \sigma^2/L]$$

$$E[x(t)n(t)\bar{d}] = n(t)^2[\mu^2 + \sigma^2/L]$$

Thereby,

$$E\left(\left[x(t) - n(t)\bar{d}\right]^2\right) = \sigma^2\left[L^2 - \sum n(t)^2\right]/L$$

Replacing σ^2 with s_d^2, the estimate of the variance becomes:

$$s_d^2 = \sum_{t=1}^{N}\left[x(t) - n(t)\bar{d}\right]^2 L \Big/ \left[L^2 - \sum_{t=1}^{N} n(t)^2\right]$$

since the expected value is unbiased as shown below.

$$E\left[s_d^2\right] = E\left\{\sum_{t=1}^{N}\left[x(t) - n(t)\bar{d}\right]^2 L \Big/ \left[L^2 - \sum_{t=1}^{N} n(t)^2\right]\right\} = \sigma^2$$

Summary

Prior to forecasting, the history of monthly demands are filtered seeking out any outlier demands, and if found, the outliers are adjusted accordingly. Filtering is not easy, but is important to generate forecasts with minimal forecast error. The filtering methods described here are developed when the demands follow a horizontal demand pattern, a trend demand pattern and a seasonal demand pattern. Another phase of filtering the demands, occurs in the order entry of the inventory location. This is when the orders come in from customers and the purchase order states a part number and quantity. The quantity is verified to be statistically consistent with those from the part's history of demands. Any line demand detected as an outlier is sent back to the customer for verification.

Chapter 10
Standard Normal and Truncated Normal Distributions

10.1 Introduction

The normal distribution is perhaps the most commonly used probability distribution in materials management as well as in many other scientific developments. This chapter shows how the variable x, from the normal, is related to the standard normal distribution with variable z. A portion of the standard normal contains all values of $(z>k)$ where k is a specific value of z. Of particular interest in subsequent use is the partial mean and partial standard deviation of the measure $(z-k)$ from this portion of the standard normal. Another useful distribution is the truncated normal that also is defined with a parameter k. This distribution has many shapes and a measure of interest is the coefficient of variation, cov, that helps to identify the shape of the distribution. The two distributions, standard normal and truncated normal, have applications in inventory control and examples on how they are used appears in Chaps. 11 and 12.

10.2 Normal Distribution

A variable x with a normal distribution has a mean μ, standard deviation σ, and is labeled as: $x \sim N(\mu, \sigma^2)$. The distribution appears as bell shaped as depicted in Fig. 10.1. The range of x is almost always from $(\mu-3\sigma)$ to $(\mu+3\sigma)$ and the most likely value is μ.

N. T. *Thomopoulos, Demand Forecasting for Inventory Control,*
DOI 10.1007/978-3-319-11976-2_10

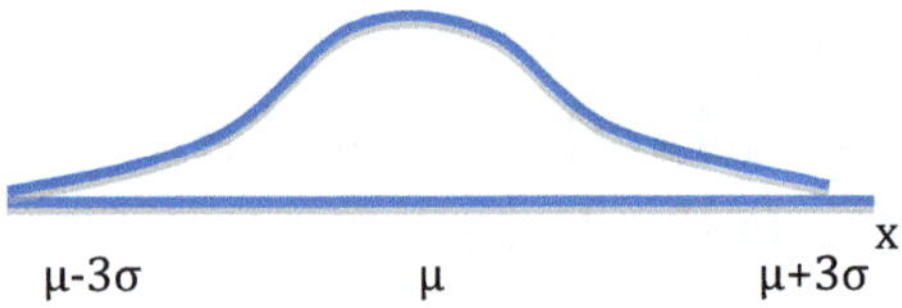

Fig. 10.1 The normal distribution of $x \sim N(\mu, \sigma^2)$

10.3 Standard Normal Distribution

A companion distribution is the standard normal distribution with variable z that has a mean of zero, standard deviation of one, and thereby is denoted as: $z \sim N(0, 1)$. The variable z is related to x in the following way:

$$z = (x - \mu)/\sigma$$

and

$$x = \mu + z\sigma$$

10.3.1 Probability Density

If k is a particular value of z, the probability density at z=k, denoted as f(k), is

$$f(k) = 1/\sqrt{2\pi}\, e^{-k^2/2}$$

10.3.2 Cumulative Distribution Function

The cumulative probability distribution at z=k is the following;

$$F(k) = \int_{-\infty}^{k} f(z)dz$$

This is the probability that z is less or equal to k.

The complement of F(k) is noted as H(k), the probability of z larger than k, and is obtained as follows:

$$H(k) = \int_{k}^{\infty} f(z)dz$$
$$= 1 - F(k)$$

Figure 10.2 shows the relation of z, k, f(k), F(k) and H(k).

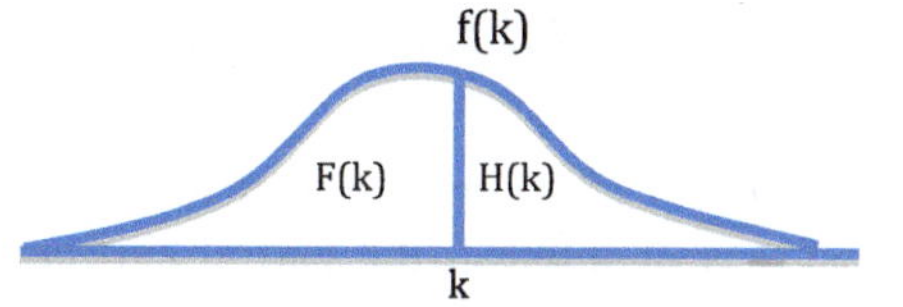

Fig. 10.2 Some measures from the standard normal distribution

10.4 Partial Measures

The partial measures of the standard normal depend on a parameter k, a particular value of the random variable z. Of importance is the portion of the standard normal that is larger than k, whereby the variable is denoted as (z>k). Of particular interest is the mean and standard deviation of (z>k). These are denoted as $\mu_p(k)$ and $\sigma_p(k)$, respectively. The mean is commonly referred as the partial expectation and labeled as E(z>k) for which, $\mu_p(k)=E(z>k)$, and the standard deviation is called the partial standard deviation. These measures are used in inventory control applications as described in Chaps. 11 and 12.

10.4.1 Partial Expectation

The partial expectation of z-greater-than-k is here denoted at E(z>k). This measures is derived as follows:

$$E(z > k) = \int_k^\infty (z-k) f(z) dz$$

For notational ease, the mean of the partial normal is labeled here as $\mu_p(k)$, where,

$$\mu_p(k) = E(z > k)$$

10.4.2 Partial Standard Deviation

The partial variance with parameter k is also a useful measure in subsequent analysis. This is computed by,

$$\sigma_p(k)^2 = E\left[(z > k)^2\right] - \left[E(z > k)\right]^2$$

where,

$$E\left[(z > k)^2\right] = \int_k^\infty (z-k)^2 f(z) dz$$

The partial standard deviation is simply $\sigma_p(k)$.

10.4.3 Partial When $(x>x_o)$

In the event x is normally distributed with $x \sim N(\mu, \sigma^2)$, and a partial measure of $(x>x_o)$ is of interest, the partial expectation, variance and standard deviation of $(x>x_o)$ are obtained as below. First note that $k=[x_o-\mu]/\sigma$.

$$E(x > x_o) = E(z > k)\sigma$$

$$V(x > x_o) = V(z > k)\sigma^2$$

and,

$$\sigma_{(x>x_o)} = \sigma_P(k)\sigma$$

10.4.4 Table Measures

Table 10.1 lists selected values from the standard normal distribution [k, F(k), H(k), f(k)], and related partial measures $[\mu_P(k), \sigma_P(k)]$. The final three columns list values from the truncated normal distribution, $[\mu_T(k), \sigma_T(k), c_T(k)]$, which are described subsequently.

10.5 Truncated Normal Distribution

Consider the truncated standard normal distribution with k a location parameter where only the values of z greater than k are included. Another variable, t, is defined where $t=z-k$ and $t>0$. The probability density of t with parameter k is here denoted as $g_k(t)$ where,

$$g_k(t) = f(z)/H(k) \quad t > 0 \text{ and } t = z - k$$

For a particular value of t, say t_1, the corresponding value of z is $z_1=t_1+k$. The cumulative probability of t_1, denoted as $G_k(t_1)$, is obtained from,

$$G_k(t_1) = \int_0^{t1} g_k(t)\,dt$$

The truncated expectancies, E(t) and $E(t^2)$, are obtained as below:

$$E(t) = \int_0^{\infty} t g_k(t)\,dt$$

$$E(t^2) = \int_0^{\infty} t^2 g_k(t)\,dt$$

Table 10.1 Some statistics from the Standard Normal Distribution, [F(k), H(k,), f(k)], Partial Measures, [$\mu_P(k)$, $\sigma_P(k)$], and from the Truncated Normal Distribution [$\mu_T(k)$, $\sigma_T(k)$, $c_T(k)$]

K	F(k)	H(k)	f(k)	$\mu_P(k)$	$\sigma_P(k)$	$\mu_T(k)$	$\sigma_T(k)$	$c_T(k)$
−3.0	0.001	0.999	0.004	3.000	0.999	3.004	0.993	0.331
−2.9	0.002	0.998	0.006	2.901	0.998	2.906	0.991	0.341
−2.8	0.003	0.997	0.008	2.801	0.998	2.808	0.989	0.352
−2.7	0.003	0.997	0.010	2.701	0.997	2.710	0.986	0.364
−2.6	0.005	0.995	0.014	2.601	0.996	2.614	0.982	0.376
−2.5	0.006	0.994	0.018	2.502	0.994	2.518	0.978	0.388
−2.4	0.008	0.992	0.022	2.403	0.993	2.423	0.972	0.401
−2.3	0.011	0.989	0.028	2.304	0.990	2.329	0.966	0.415
−2.2	0.014	0.986	0.035	2.205	0.988	2.236	0.959	0.429
−2.1	0.018	0.982	0.044	2.106	0.984	2.145	0.951	0.443
−2.0	0.023	0.977	0.054	2.008	0.980	2.055	0.942	0.458
−1.9	0.029	0.971	0.066	1.911	0.975	1.968	0.931	0.473
−1.8	0.036	0.964	0.079	1.814	0.969	1.882	0.920	0.489
−1.7	0.045	0.955	0.094	1.718	0.961	1.798	0.907	0.504
−1.6	0.055	0.945	0.111	1.623	0.953	1.717	0.894	0.520
−1.5	0.067	0.933	0.130	1.529	0.943	1.639	0.879	0.536
−1.4	0.081	0.919	0.150	1.437	0.931	1.563	0.863	0.552
−1.3	0.097	0.903	0.171	1.346	0.918	1.490	0.847	0.569
−1.2	0.115	0.885	0.194	1.256	0.902	1.419	0.830	0.585
−1.1	0.136	0.864	0.218	1.169	0.886	1.352	0.812	0.601
−1.0	0.159	0.841	0.242	1.083	0.867	1.288	0.794	0.616
−0.9	0.184	0.816	0.266	1.000	0.846	1.226	0.775	0.632
−0.8	0.212	0.788	0.290	0.920	0.823	1.168	0.756	0.647
−0.7	0.242	0.758	0.312	0.843	0.799	1.112	0.736	0.662
−0.6	0.274	0.726	0.333	0.769	0.772	1.059	0.717	0.677
−0.5	0.309	0.691	0.352	0.698	0.744	1.009	0.697	0.691
−0.4	0.345	0.655	0.368	0.630	0.714	0.962	0.678	0.705
−0.3	0.382	0.618	0.381	0.567	0.683	0.917	0.659	0.718
−0.2	0.421	0.579	0.391	0.507	0.651	0.875	0.640	0.731
−0.1	0.460	0.540	0.397	0.451	0.618	0.835	0.621	0.744
0.0	0.500	0.500	0.399	0.399	0.584	0.798	0.603	0.756
0.1	0.540	0.460	0.397	0.351	0.549	0.763	0.585	0.767
0.2	0.579	0.421	0.391	0.307	0.515	0.729	0.568	0.778
0.3	0.618	0.382	0.381	0.267	0.481	0.698	0.551	0.789
0.4	0.655	0.345	0.368	0.230	0.446	0.669	0.534	0.799
0.5	0.691	0.309	0.352	0.198	0.413	0.641	0.518	0.808
0.6	0.726	0.274	0.333	0.169	0.380	0.615	0.503	0.817
0.7	0.758	0.242	0.312	0.143	0.349	0.590	0.488	0.826

Table 10.1 (continued)

K	F(k)	H(k)	f(k)	$\mu_P(k)$	$\sigma_P(k)$	$\mu_T(k)$	$\sigma_T(k)$	$c_T(k)$
0.8	0.788	0.212	0.290	0.120	0.318	0.567	0.473	0.834
0.9	0.816	0.184	0.266	0.100	0.289	0.546	0.460	0.842
1.0	0.841	0.159	0.242	0.083	0.262	0.525	0.446	0.850
1.1	0.864	0.136	0.218	0.069	0.236	0.506	0.433	0.857
1.2	0.885	0.115	0.194	0.056	0.211	0.488	0.421	0.863
1.3	0.903	0.097	0.171	0.046	0.189	0.470	0.409	0.870
1.4	0.919	0.081	0.150	0.037	0.168	0.454	0.398	0.876
1.5	0.933	0.067	0.130	0.029	0.148	0.439	0.387	0.882
1.6	0.945	0.055	0.111	0.023	0.131	0.424	0.376	0.887
1.7	0.955	0.045	0.094	0.018	0.115	0.410	0.366	0.892
1.8	0.964	0.036	0.079	0.014	0.100	0.397	0.356	0.897
1.9	0.971	0.029	0.066	0.011	0.087	0.385	0.347	0.902
2.0	0.977	0.023	0.054	0.008	0.075	0.373	0.338	0.906
2.1	0.982	0.018	0.044	0.006	0.065	0.362	0.330	0.910
2.2	0.986	0.014	0.035	0.005	0.056	0.351	0.321	0.914
2.3	0.989	0.011	0.028	0.004	0.048	0.341	0.313	0.918
2.4	0.992	0.008	0.022	0.003	0.041	0.332	0.306	0.921
2.5	0.994	0.006	0.018	0.002	0.035	0.323	0.298	0.924
2.6	0.995	0.005	0.014	0.001	0.029	0.314	0.291	0.926
2.7	0.997	0.003	0.010	0.001	0.025	0.306	0.284	0.928
2.8	0.997	0.003	0.008	0.001	0.021	0.298	0.277	0.929
2.9	0.998	0.002	0.006	0.001	0.017	0.291	0.270	0.931
3.0	0.999	0.001	0.004	0.000	0.014	0.283	0.264	0.933

10.5.1 Truncated Mean and Variance

For notational consistency, the truncated mean and variance are denoted as: $\mu_T(k)$ and $\sigma_T(k)^2$, respectively, and are obtained as below:

$$\mu_T(k) = E(t)$$

$$\sigma_T(k)^2 = E(t^2) - E(t)^2$$

Note, the truncated standard deviation is simply $\sigma_T(k)$.

10.5.2 Some Useful Identities

The following identities are useful in the calculations.

$$H(k) = 1 - F(k)$$

$$E(z > k) = f(k) - kH(k)$$

$$E\left[(z > k)^2\right] = H(k)(1+k^2) - kf(k)$$

$$E(t) = E(z > k) / H(k)$$

$$E(t^2) = E\left[(z > k)^2\right]/H(k)$$

$$\mu_T(k) = E(t)$$

10.5.3 Truncated Cov

A convenient way to identify the truncated normal distribution is by the coefficient of variation, cov, computed by,

$$\text{cov} = \sigma_T(k) / \mu_T(k)$$

For notational ease, the truncated coefficient of variation with parameter k is labeled here as $c_T(k)$, whereby,

$$c_T(k) = \text{cov}.$$

Table 10.2 lists various values of the cov (0.3 to 1.0) from the truncated normal distribution with their associate parameter k and measure H(k). When cov is 0.50 or less, the shape of the distribution is much like the standard normal distribution. When cov is 0.90 or larger, the distribution looks like an exponential distribution.

Figure 10.3 depicts the truncated normal distribution when cov = 0.3, 0.5, 0.7 and 0.9. The corresponding parameters k are approximately −3.5, −1.7, −0.4 and 1.9, respectively. Note at cov = 0.5 or less, the truncated normal appears much like the

Table 10.2 The truncated normal distribution with selected values of cov and associated values of k and H(k)

Cov	k	H(k)
0.3	−3.5	1.000
0.4	−2.4	0.992
0.5	−1.7	0.955
0.6	−1.1	0.864
0.7	−0.4	0.655
0.8	0.4	0.345
0.9	1.9	0.029
1.0	3.5	0.000

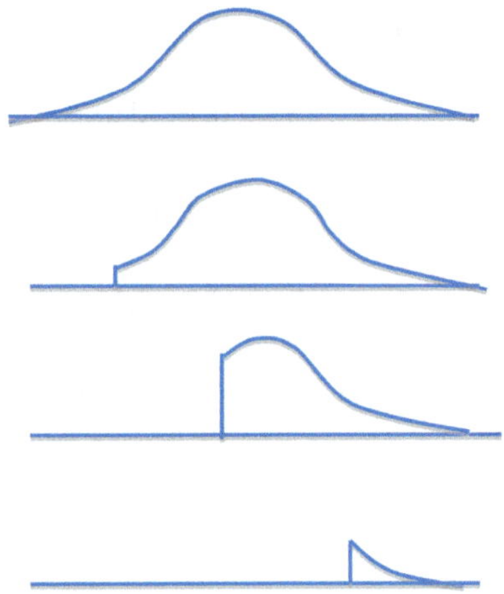

Fig. 10.3 Truncated normal at $c_T(k)=cov=0.3$, 0.5, 0.7 and 0.9

standard normal. When cov is 0.9 or larger, the distribution is like an exponential distribution, far from the standard normal.

Example 10.1 Consider the variable x that follows a normal distribution with parameters, $\mu=10$ and $\sigma=2$. Hence, $x \sim N(10, 2^2)$. Now assume the probability of x larger than $x_o=9$ is of interest to an analyst. Note, the corresponding values from the standard normal are as below:

$$\begin{aligned} k &= (x_o - \mu)/\sigma \\ &= (9-10)/2 \\ &= -0.5 \end{aligned}$$

Thereby, from Table 10.1,

$$H(-0.5) = 0.691$$

is the probability of $x>9$.

Example 10.2 Suppose the analyst is now interested in the partial variable $(x>9)$ and also the associated mean and standard deviation of the partial variable. From the standard normal, the parameter becomes,

$$k = (9-10)/2 = -0.5$$

Scanning Table 10.1 at $k=-0.5$, yields $\mu_p(k)=0.698$ and $\sigma_p(k)=0.744$. Thereby,

$$\begin{aligned} E(x>9) &= E(z>k)\sigma \\ &= \mu_P(k)\sigma \\ &= 0.698 \times 2 \\ &= 1.396 \end{aligned}$$

$$\sigma_{(x>9)} = \sigma_p(k)\sigma$$
$$= 0.744 \times 2$$
$$= 1.488$$

So, the partial mean of (x>9) is 1.396 and the associated partial standard deviation is 1.488.

Example 10.3 Assume now, the analyst is interested in measuring the coefficient of variation from the truncated distribution with x larger than $x_o = 9$. This measure can be obtained from the corresponding standard truncated normal distribution with parameter k. From the standard normal, the parameter becomes,

$$k = (9 - 10) / 2 = 0.5$$

Now pursuing the truncated measures in Table 10.1 with parameter $k = -0.5$, the mean is $\mu_T(-0.5) = 1.009$; the standard deviation is $\sigma_T(k) = 0.697$; and the coefficient of variation is $c_T(k) = 0.697/1.009 = 0.691$. Thereby, the coefficient of variation for the truncated normal with (x>9) is cov = 0.691.

10.5.4 Three Related Variables: z, t and w

Now consider another variable, w, that is related to the variables t and z as shown below:

Let,

$$t = \mu_T(k) + w\sigma_T(k)$$

and

$$w = [t - \mu_T(k)] / \sigma_T(k)$$

Note also, since, $t = (z - k)$,

$$w = [z - k - \mu_T(k)] / \sigma_T(k)$$

For a particular value of t, say, t_o, there are corresponding values z_o and w_o as shown below,

$$z_o = t_o + k$$

$$w_o = [z_o - k - \mu_T(k)] / \sigma_T(k)$$

Below shows the relation with the partial expectations of the three variables. Recall Table 10.1 where a given cov yields a unique location parameter k. Now for a given cov, k and ($t_o > 0$),

$$E(t > t_o) = E(z > z_o) / H(k)$$

and

$$E(w > w_o) = E(t > t_o) / \sigma_T(k)$$
$$= E(z > z_o) / [H(k)\sigma_T(k)]$$

Also,

$$E(z > z_o) = E(w > w_o)[H(k)\sigma_T(k)]$$

10.5.5 Limits on w

The limits on the variable w can be derived now. Recall,

$$w = [z - k - \mu_T(k)] / \sigma_T(k)$$

where k is the location parameter on z. When z=k,

$$w = -\mu_T(k) / \sigma_T(k)$$
$$= -1 / c_T(k)$$

Hence, the interval on the random variable w becomes,

$$-1 / c_T(k) < w < \infty$$

Note, for example when the coefficient of variation is: $c_T(k)$=cov=(0.33, 0.50, 1.00), the limits are as listed below:

Cov	w-interval
0.33	$-3.00 < w < \infty$
0.50	$-2.00 < w < \infty$
1.00	$-1.00 < w < \infty$

The relations shown here between random variables t, z and w will be useful in developing the safety stock applications of Chap. 11.

10.5.6 Hastings Approximations

There is no closed-form solution for the cumulative distribution F(z). A way to approximate F(z) has been developed by C. Hastings, Jr. Two methods credited to Hastings are listed below.

10.5.7 Approximation of F(z) from z

For a given z, to find F(z), the following Hastings routine is run.

1. $d_1 = 0.0498673470$

   $d_2 = 0.0211410061$

   $d_3 = 0.0032776263$

   $d_4 = 0.0000380036$

   $d_5 = 0.0000488906$

   $d_6 = 0.0000053830$

2. If $z \geq 0, k = z$

   If $z < 0, k = -z$

3. $F = 1 - 0.5\left[1 + d_1 k + d_2 k^2 + d_3 k^3 + d_4 k^4 + d_5 k^5 + d_6 k^6\right]^{-16}$

4. if $z \geq 0,\ F(z) = F$

   If $z < 0, F(z) = 1 - F$

Return F(z).

10.5.8 Approximation of z from F(z)

Another useful approximation also comes from Hastings, and gives a formula that yields a random z from a value of F(z). The routine is listed below.

1. $c_0 = 2.515517$
   $c_1 = 0.802853$
   $c_2 = 0.010328$
   $d_1 = 1.432788$
   $d_2 = 0.189269$
   $d_3 = 0.001308$
2. $H(z) = 1 - F(z)$
   If $H(z) \leq 0.5,\ H = H(z)$
   If $H(z) > 0.5, H = 1 - H(z)$
3. $t = \sqrt{\ln(1/H^2)}$ where ln = natural logarithm.
4. $k = t - \left[c_0 + c_1 t + c_2 t^2\right] / \left[1 + d_1 t + d_2 t^2 + d_3 t^3\right]$
5. If $H(z) \leq 0.5,\ z = k$

If $H(z) > 0.5,\ z = -k$

Return z.

Summary

The normal distribution with random variable, x, is defined along with its mean and standard deviation. The normal is related to the standard normal distribution with random variable z, and where table values are listed in almost all statistical books. The standard normal is also related to the partial measures that are defined here with parameter k and includes the portion of the distribution where (z>k). The standard normal is also related to the truncated normal with parameter k and includes only the values of (z>k). The coefficient of variation from the truncated normal is of particular interest. Table values are listed with measures from the standard normal distribution, partial measures, and truncated normal distribution. Two approximations are also given which allow the user to measure F(z) from z, and z from F(z), where F(z) is the cumulative distribution of the standard normal.

Chapter 11
Safety Stock

11.1 Introduction

Safety stock is the extra inventory to hold for an item for protection against demands exceeding the forecast. This type of stock concerns entities where the demands of the future are not known until they happen, like in distribution centers, stores and dealers. In plants, where the production schedules are set in advance, safety stock is usually not needed. The typical way to measure the variability in the forecasts is by the standard deviation of the one month ahead forecast error. A relative measure is the coefficient of variation. Two common methods of generating the safety stock are: the service level (probability not out of stock), and the percent fill (ratio of demand filled over total demand) methods. Both methods are also sometimes referred as the service level method. The normal distribution is used primarily to generate how much safety stock to have available. This chapter shows how the truncated normal distribution can also serve this function. The truncated normal has many shapes and includes only portions of the right-hand-side of the standard normal.

11.2 Control of the Inventory

The amount of inventory to carry is computed to comply with management's desire of service to the customers. The goal is to have enough stock to satisfy the demands coming in from the customers. Two methods of determining the safety stock are described in this chapter, the service level method and the percent fill method. In many stocking locations, the safety stock consists of almost half of the total inventory. The primary desire of the inventory management is to have the least amount of inventory to satisfy the demands of the customers. The safety stock is needed because of the uncertainty in the forecasts. The more accurate the forecasts, the less safety stock is needed, and thereby, the less inventory.

N. T. Thomopoulos, *Demand Forecasting for Inventory Control*,
DOI 10.1007/978-3-319-11976-2_11

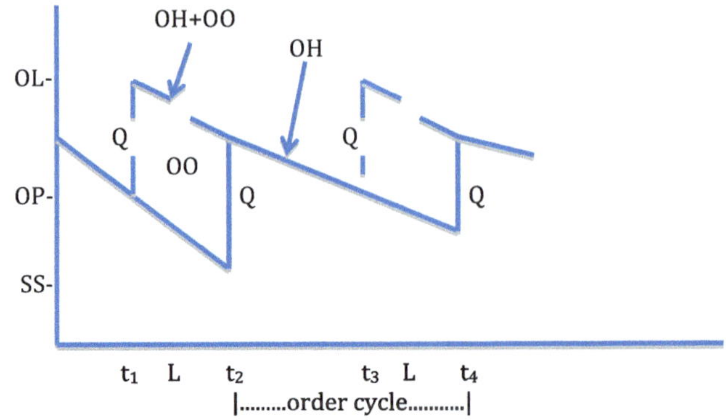

Fig. 11.1 On-hand and on-order flow for a continuous review inventory system

Customer service is defined in many ways, depending on the role by which the inventory is used. The two most common interpretations are the following: (1) the probability the demand over the lead time does not exceed the inventory on-hand, and (2) the ratio of demand filled from stock on-hand over the total demand. More on these are described below. A good inventory system is one where the level of customer service is high and the amount of inventory is at the minimum possible.

It is common to refer to the total inventory as total stock (TS). The total stock is partitioned into two components: cycle stock (CS) and safety stock (SS). The cycle stock is needed to fill the forecast of demands from the customers, and the safety stock is needed in the event the demands exceed the forecasts.

A common way to control the inventory on each item in the stocking location is by the order point, OP, and order level, OL. Figure 11.1 depicts how this works. At time t_1, the on-hand, OH, plus on-order, OO, inventory reaches the OP, and this triggers the system to buy new inventory of size Q to reach the OL. This new inventory is OO that is shown with a dotted line. The OH inventory is depicted with a solid line. The order Q will be received a lead time, L, later at $t_2 = t_1 + L$. At t_3, the OH + OO again falls to the OP and a new replenishment of stock of size Q is ordered. This stock is received at time $t_4 = t_3 + L$. The time between two receipts of stock, t_2 to t_4, is called the order cycle.

This chapter describes the two main methods of generating the safety stock: the service level method and the percent fill method.

11.3 Safety Stock when Normal Distribution

This section shows how to generate the safety stock with the assumption the monthly demands follow a normal distribution, where the mean is the monthly forecast and the variation is the standard deviation of the one month forecast error.

11.4 Service Level Method

A common way to determine the safety stock is by the service level method. The management sets a parameter, SL, that specifies the probability the demand over the lead-time will not exceed the amount of stock available. With this method two measures are computed, the order point, OP, and the order level, OL, as follows:

$$OP = F_L + SS$$
$$OL = OP + Q$$

where, F_L = forecast of the demands over the lead time, SS = safety stock and Q = order quantity. All three of these quantities come from the forecasts of the future months, $F(\tau)\ \tau = 1, 2, \ldots$ The computations for the safety stock is shown below.

The lead-time forecast, F_L, is computed as,

$$\begin{aligned} F_L &= L \times F(1) && \text{if } L \leq 1 \\ &= F(1) + (L-1) \times F(2) && \text{if } 1 < L \leq 2 \end{aligned}$$

and so forth.

The safety stock is obtained from the normal distribution, the standard deviation of the one-month ahead forecast error, σ, and the lead-time, L. The lead time is the length of time between ordering replenish stock till receiving the stock. The standard deviation over the lead-time, σ_L, is obtained by,

$$\sigma_L = \sqrt{L}\,\sigma$$

The parameter SL is set to the cumulative probability in the standard normal distribution, F(k) and k is called the safety factor. That is,

$$F(k) = SL$$

where k is the value of z, from the standard normal, where $P(z \leq k) = F(k) = SL$. So, the safety stock becomes,

$$SS = k\sigma_L$$

The order quantity, Q, is the amount of stock to order for replenishment. This quantity is determined by an economic analysis using the forecast of the future months as well as the costs associated with buying and holding the stock. With each new order quantity, the on-order, OO, increases by Q; and when the stock arrives, the OO decreases by Q and the on-hand, OH, increases by Q.

The on-hand, OH, plus on-order, OO, inventory is monitored daily with the order point, OP, to determine when and how much to buy as described below.

$$\begin{aligned} &\text{If } (OH + OO) > OP && \text{buy} = 0 \\ &\text{If } (OH + OO) \leq OP && \text{buy} = OL - (OH + OO) \end{aligned}$$

The buy quantity is placed when (OH + OO) falls equal or below the OP mark.

Example 11.1 Consider a part with horizontal forecasts of F = 100 for each of the future months, and a standard deviation of $\sigma = 30$. Suppose the lead time is L = 2 months, the order quantity is Q = 100 pieces, and the management sets the service level at SL = 0.95. For this scenario, the following computations take place:

$$F_L = 2 \times 100 = 200$$
$$\sigma_L = \sqrt{2} \times 30 = 42.4$$
$$k = 1.65 \quad (\text{since } F(1.65) \approx 0.95 \quad \text{from Table 10.1})$$
$$SS = 1.65 \times 42.4 = 69.96 \approx 70$$
$$OP = 200 + 70 = 270$$
$$OL = 270 + 100 = 370$$

Each day, the sum (OH + OO) is compared with the OP, and if (OH + OO) ≤ 270, the replenish quantity becomes: buy = 370– (OH + OO).

11.5 Percent Fill Method

Another common way to determine the safety stock, SS, with the normal distribution, is by the percent fill method, sometimes called the service level method. This method measures the percent fill (PF), as:

$$PF = (\text{demand filled}) / (\text{total demand})$$

The management sets the PF desired and the method determines the order point, OP, and order level, OL needed to accomplish. This method requires the following data: the monthly forecasts, $F(\tau)$ $\tau = 1, 2, \ldots$, the lead-time (month), L, the one month standard deviation, σ, the order quantity, Q, and the desired percent fill, PF. The forecast for the lead-time is F_L, and the associated standard deviation over the lead-time is obtained by,

$$\sigma_L = \sqrt{L}\sigma$$

To find the safety factor, a time interval is needed that allows the computations to take place. The time duration covering the order cycle, OC, is selected, and the PF for this duration is set as the desired percent fill. The order cycle is the time interval between two receipts of new stock. For this length of time, the percent fill is:

$$\begin{aligned} PF &= (\text{demand filled in OC})/(\text{total demand in OC}) \\ &= 1 - (\text{demand short in OC})/(\text{total demand in OC}). \\ &= 1 - E(z > k)\sigma_L / Q \end{aligned}$$

Note, Q is the amount of replenish stock in the order cycle and represents the expected demand in the OC; and $E(z>k)\sigma_L$ is the expected demand exceeding the OP during the order cycle, and therefore is a measure of the stock that is short in the OC. So now, the partial expectation becomes,

$$E(z > k) = (1 - PF)Q/\sigma_L$$

The safety factor, k, that corresponds to $E(z>k)$ is obtained from Table 10.1. Note from the table where $k>0$ only when $E(z>k)<0.40$. To avoid a negative safety stock, k is set to zero when $E(z>k) \geq 0.40$, whereby no safety stock is needed.

With k now obtained, the safety stock is computed by,

$$SS = k\sigma_L$$

The order point, OP, and order level, OL, become,

$$OP = F_L + SS$$
$$OL = OP + Q$$

Each day the sum (OH + OO) is compared to the OP and if (OH + OO) $\leq$OP, a new buy quantity, buy, is needed and becomes,

$$buy = OL - (OH + OO)$$

In this way, the inventory replenishments for the item is controlled to yield the percent fill, PF, desired by the management.

Example 11.2 Suppose a part where the management wants a percent fill of $PF=0.95$. Assume the horizontal forecast is $F=100$ per future month, the standard deviation is $\sigma=30$, the lead-time is $L=2$ months, and the order quantity is $Q=100$ pieces. For this situation, the following computations take place.

$$F_L = 2 \times 100 = 200$$
$$\sigma_L = \sqrt{2} \times 30 = 42.4$$
$$E(z > k) = (1 - 0.95)100 / 42.4 = 0.118$$

Table 10.1 shows: $E(z>0.8)=0.120$ and $E(z>0.9)=0.100$. Using interpolation,

$$\begin{aligned} k &= 0.80 + [E(z > k) - E(z > 0.8)] \times [0.9 - 0.8]/[E(z > 0.9) - E(z > 0.8)] \\ &= 0.80 + [0.118 - 0.120] \times [0.9 - 0.8]/[0.100 - 0.120] \\ &= 0.82 \end{aligned}$$

Thereby,

$$SS = 0.82 \times 42.4 = 34.77 \approx 35$$
$$OP = 200 + 35 = 235$$
$$OL = 235 + 100 = 335$$

11.6 Sensitivity of Safety Stock with Cov

The accuracy of the forecast is measured by the standard deviation of the one-month ahead forecast error, σ. A relative measure is the coefficient of variation, cov = σ/F, where F is the average one month forecast. The lower the cov, the more accurate the forecast, and the less safety stock is needed. Below shows how much safety stock can be reduced with a relative decrease in the forecast error measured by, σ or cov.

11.7 Service Level Safety Stock and Cov

When the service level method is used, the safety stock is generated by,

$$SS = k\sigma\sqrt{L}$$

where σ is the standard deviation, k is the safety factor, and L is the lead time in months. The only ingredient that is affected by the forecast accuracy is the standard deviation. Thereby, a 10 % decrease in the standard deviation will lower the safety stock needs by 10 %. In the same way, a 10 % decrease in the cov will lower the safety stock by 10 %. In essence, the more accurate the forecast, the lower the inventory to satisfy management's desire of customer service.

11.8 Percent Fill Safety Stock and Cov

When the percent fill method is used to find the safety stock, the relation between the cov and the safety stock is not straight forward, as in the service level method. Recall, the partial expectation is computed as below,

$$E(z > k) = (1 - PF)Q / \left(\sigma\sqrt{L}\right)$$

where, PF is the percent fill desired, Q is the order quantity, σ is the one month standard deviation and L is the lead-time in months.

In a generic way, when F = the average one month forecast, Q = M × F is the order quantity where M is the months-in-buy, and σ = cov × F. The partial expectation becomes,

$$E(z > k) = (1 - PF)M/\left(cov\sqrt{L}\right)$$

and thereby E(z>k) depends on the four generic ingredients: PF, M, cov and L

For a particular item in the inventory, the value of E(z>k) is computed and a search is needed to find the corresponding safety factor, k, whereby, the safety stock quantity becomes,

$$SS = k\sigma\sqrt{L}$$

Months of Safety Stock

It is helpful to transform the safety stock quantity into months supply terms, denoted as, ss. Note, SS = ss × F where SS is safety stock in pieces and ss is safety stock in months supply. Recall, cov = σ/F. The measure for months supply is below.

$$ss = k \times cov\sqrt{L}$$

Table 11.1 gives the months of safety stock needed for five levels of percent fill (0.90, 0.925, 0.95, 0.975, 0.99), and five values of the cov (0.30, 0.50, 0.60, 0.80, 1.00). The table also give five combinations, (L, M), of lead-time (months), L, and months-in-buy, M: (0.5, 0.5), (0.5, 1.0), (1.0, 1.0), (1.0, 2.0), (2.0, 1.0). Note, for example, when PF = 0.95, L = 1, M = 2 and cov = 0.6, the months of safety stock needed is 0.36.

The right-hand-side of the table gives the percent reduction in months of safety stock when the cov reduces by 10%. For example, consider the table values listed below:

PF	L	M	cov	ss
0.95	1.0	2.0	0.60	0.36
0.95	1.0	2.0	0.80	0.62

The percent change in cov is (0.80 − 0.60)/0.80 = 0.250 (25.0%).

The percent change in months of safety stock is: (0.62 − 0.36)/0.62 = 0.419 (41.9%)

So, 0.419/0.250 = 1.676 is the percent change in months of safety stock with a one percent reduction in the cov. Using 10% as the base, when the cov = 0.8 is reduced by 10%, the corresponding reduction in the safety stock months is 16.8%. This illustrates how the 10% entries of Table 11.1 are derived.

Table 11.1 Months of safety stock by percent fill (PF), when lead time months, L, months-in-buy, M, and coefficient of variation, cov; and percent reduction in safety stock for a 10 % reduction in cov

Months of safety stock								Percent reduction in SS when 10 % reduction in cov			
Cov								Cov			
PF	L	M	0.3	0.5	0.6	0.8	1.0	0.5	0.6	0.8	1.0
0.90	0.5	0.5	0.08	0.25	0.34	0.55	0.77	17.0	15.9	15.3	14.3
	0.5	1.0	0.00	0.09	0.16	0.32	0.50	25.0	26.4	20.0	18.0
	1.0	1.0	0.04	0.24	0.36	0.62	0.90	20.8	20.1	16.8	15.6
	1.0	2.0	0.00	0.00	0.08	0.27	0.49	—	60.2	28.1	22.4
	2.0	1.0	0.16	0.50	0.69	1.09	1.53	17.0	16.6	14.7	14.4
0.925	0.5	0.5	0.12	0.31	0.41	0.63	0.87	15.3	14.7	14.0	13.8
	0.5	1.0	0.02	0.16	0.24	0.42	0.61	21.9	20.1	17.1	15.6
	1.0	1.0	0.10	0.33	0.47	0.75	1.05	17.4	17.9	14.9	14.3
	1.0	2.0	0.00	0.11	0.20	0.42	0.67	25.0	27.1	21.0	18.7
	2.0	1.0	0.24	0.61	0.82	1.26	1.73	15.2	15.4	14.0	13.6
0.95	0.5	0.5	0.17	0.38	0.50	0.74	1.00	13.8	14.5	13.0	13.0
	0.5	1.0	0.08	0.25	0.34	0.55	0.77	17.0	15.9	15.3	14.3
	1.0	1.0	0.18	0.45	0.60	0.92	1.25	15.0	15.1	13.9	13.2
	1.0	2.0	0.04	0.24	0.36	0.62	0.90	20.8	20.1	16.8	15.6
	2.0	1.0	0.34	0.77	1.00	1.48	2.00	14.0	13.9	13.0	13.0
0.975	0.5	0.5	0.25	0.50	0.63	0.92	1.21	12.5	12.4	12.6	12.0
	0.5	1.0	0.17	0.38	0.50	0.74	1.00	13.8	14.5	13.0	13.0
	1.0	1.0	0.30	0.63	0.80	1.18	1.57	13.1	12.8	12.9	12.4
	1.0	2.0	0.18	0.45	0.60	0.92	1.25	15.0	15.1	13.9	13.2
	2.0	1.0	0.50	1.00	1.27	1.83	2.42	12.5	12.8	12.2	12.2
0.99	0.5	0.5	0.34	0.64	0.79	1.12	1.46	11.7	11.4	11.8	11.6
	0.5	1.0	0.27	0.53	0.68	0.97	1.27	12.3	13.3	12.0	11.8
	1.0	1.0	0.43	0.83	1.04	1.48	1.94	12.0	12.2	11.9	11.9
	1.0	2.0	0.33	0.68	0.86	1.25	1.66	12.9	12.6	12.5	12.3
	2.0	1.0	0.68	1.27	1.59	2.24	2.92	11.6	12.1	11.6	11.6

11.9 Safety Stock when Truncated Normal Distribution

In Chap. 10, the truncated normal distribution is introduced; and this is the distribution used here to find the amount of safety stock needed by way of the service level method and the percent fill method. The distribution is useful in inventory control since it has many shapes that are applicable. Consider a part where the monthly forecast is labeled as F, the one month standard deviation is denoted by σ and the demands over the months are always zero or larger. Recall the coefficient of variation, cov, is measured by cov = σ/F. In the event F = 3σ, the standard deviation

Table 11.2 The truncated standard distribution with approximate values of cov, k and H(k)

Cov	k	H(k)
0.3	−3.5	1.000
0.4	−2.4	0.992
0.5	−1.7	0.955
0.6	−1.1	0.864
0.7	−0.4	0.655
0.8	0.4	0.345
0.9	1.9	0.029
1.0	3.5	0.001

is one-third the forecast and cov = σ/F = 0.33. For this situation, the shape of the demands for the month could be the same as a normal since all the demands are zero or larger and the probability of a demand below zero is nil. For any part with cov ≤ 0.33, the normal assumption is possible since the probability of all demands larger than zero is near one.

When cov = 1.00, however, the shape of the monthly demands are more like an exponential distribution, and are sometimes referred as lumpy demands. In this situation, the normal distribution does not apply. In this scenario, the distribution of monthly demands begins at zero and is skewed far to the right of F. The normal distribution does not closely resemble this distribution. The same is true for the distributions as cov increases above the 0.33 mark.

Table 11.2 has entries that are taken from Table 10.1 of Chap. 10. When the cov from the truncated normal is 0.4, say, the associated parameter from the standard normal is k = −2.4, and H(k) = 0.992. At cov = 0.5, the associated parameter is k = −1.7,and H(k) = 0.955. Neither of these truncated normal distributions are much different that the standard normal. But when cov = 0.6, k = −1.1 and H(k) = 0.864, whereby 13.6% of the demands would fall negative, and this distribution starts to drift away from the normal. When cov = 0.7 or larger, the distribution becomes much different than a normal.

11.10 Lead Time Demand

As the forecasting system measures the average monthly forecast, F, and the corresponding one month standard deviation, σ, the coefficient of variation for one month is cov = σ/F. But in computing the amount of safety stock to have available by the availability method and the percent fill method, the distribution of the demands cover the lead-time duration, and thereby the cov for the lead-time is needed to control the inventory properly. Since,

$$F_L = F(1) + \ldots + F(L)$$

Table 11.3 Value of the lead-time coefficient of variation, covL, when the lead-time is L months, and the one month coefficient of variation is cov

L\cov	0.10	0.20	0.30	0.40	0.50	0.60	0.70	0.80	0.90	1.00
0.25	0.20	0.40	0.60	0.80	1.00	1.20	1.40	1.60	1.80	2.00
0.50	0.14	0.28	0.42	0.57	0.71	0.85	0.99	1.13	1.27	1.41
0.75	0.12	0.23	0.35	0.46	0.58	0.69	0.81	0.92	1.04	1.15
1.00	0.10	0.20	0.30	0.40	0.50	0.60	0.70	0.80	0.90	1.00
2.00	0.07	0.14	0.21	0.28	0.35	0.42	0.49	0.57	0.64	0.71
3.00	0.06	0.12	0.17	0.23	0.29	0.35	0.40	0.46	0.52	0.58
4.00	0.05	0.10	0.15	0.20	0.25	0.30	0.35	0.40	0.45	0.50

is the mean of the lead-time distribution, and

$$\sigma_L = \sqrt{L}\sigma$$

is the associated standard deviation, the coefficient of variation for the lead-time becomes,

$$cov_L = \sigma_L / F_L.$$

Table 11.3 shows how the cov_L is related to the one month cov and the lead time L. Note at L=1.00, cov_L=cov; when L<1.00, cov_L>cov; and when L>1.00, cov_L<cov. For example, when cov=0.30 (normal) and L=0.25 months, cov_L=0.60 (not normal). When cov=1.00 (not normal), and L=4 months, cov_L=0.50 (near normal), and so forth.

In stores and dealers, the lead-time is fairly low (a few days) for most items they stock, and thereby cov_L for many items in stock are high and the distribution tends to be not normally shaped. In distribution centers, the lead-time is often higher (two or more months), whereby cov_L increases and the shape of the lead-time demands approach a normal distribution.

11.11 Service Level Methods and Truncated Normal

Truncated Normal Density Consider the truncated normal with parameter k and variable t=z−k, where t≥0. The parameter k identifies the left-hand-side of the standard normal distribution where the truncation begins, and the only values of z are those greater than k. The truncated normal probability density with parameter k is:

$$g_k(t) = f(z) / H(k) \quad t \geq 0$$

The corresponding cumulative distribution of t is as follows:

$$G_k(t) = [F(z) - F(k)]/[1 - F(k)] \quad \text{for } z \geq k \text{ and } t = (z - k)$$

Example 11.3 Suppose a situation where the management wants to set the safety stock to yield the service level measure as SL = 0.90 for an item with a truncated normal distribution with $cov_L = 0.60$ and where the standard deviation for the lead time is $\sigma_L = 10$.

Table 10.1 shows when $cov_L = 0.60$, the truncated location parameter is $k = -1.1$. The table also shows that $\mu_T(-1.1) = 1.352$ and $\sigma_T(-1.1) = 0.812$. The way to find the safety factor for this scenario is given below.

$$\text{Set } G_K(t) = SL = 0.90$$

In this situation,

$$SL = [F(z) - F(k)]/[1 - F(k)]$$

and thereby,

$$F(z) = F(k) + SL \times [1 - F(k)]$$

Note from Table 10.1 where, $F(k) = F(-1.1) = 0.136$, thereby,

$$\begin{aligned} F(z_o) &= 0.136 + 0.90 \times [1 - 0.136] \\ &= 0.914 \end{aligned}$$

Referring back to Table 10.1 again, the value of z_o that yields $F(z_o) = 0.914$ is, with interpolation, $z_o = 1.36$.

Recall, $t > 0$ and $t = z - k$.

It is useful now to introduce another variable, w, where,

$$t = \mu_T(k) + w\sigma_T(k)$$

and thereby,

$$\begin{aligned} w &= [t - \mu_T(k)]/\sigma_T(k) \\ &= [z - k - \mu_T(k)]/\sigma_T(k) \end{aligned}$$

Hence, when z_o is known, the corresponding value of w, denoted as w_o, is computed as below:

$$t_o = \mu_T(k) + w_o\sigma_T(k)$$

$$w_o = [z_o - k - \mu_T(k)]/[\sigma_T(k)]$$

Continuing with Example, 11.3, $z_o = 1.36$, $k = -1.1$, $\mu_T(k) = 1.352$, $\sigma_T(k) = 0.812$, and thereby the safety factor to use is computed as below:

$$\begin{aligned} w_o &= [1.36 + 1.1 - 1.352]/0.812 \\ &= 1.36 \end{aligned}$$

Hence, the safety stock to use for this part is set as below.

$$\begin{aligned} SS &= w_o \sigma_L \\ &= 1.36 \times 10 \\ &= 13.6 \end{aligned}$$

In comparison when the normal distribution is applied, the safety factor becomes $k \approx 1.29$ via Table 10.1. The safety stock to use is computed below.

$$\begin{aligned} SS &= 1.29 \times 10 \\ &= 12.9 \end{aligned}$$

In general, the truncated safety stock will be greater or equal to the counterpart standard normal safety stock.

In summary, the steps to find the safety stock for the service level method from the truncated normal distribution are listed below:.

1. From cov_L, get k from Table 10.1.
2. Compute $F(z_o)$.
3. Find z_o from Table 10.1.
4. Compute w_o.
5. $SS = w_o \sigma_L$.

11.12 Percent Fill Method and Truncated Normal

Consider an item where the safety stock, SS, from the truncated normal is needed and the percent fill method will now be used. The data that is needed for the part is listed below:

F = one-month forecast
σ = one-month standard deviation
L = lead-time

Q = order quantity
PF = desired percent fill
$F_L = L \times F$ = lead-time forecast
$\sigma_L = \sqrt{L}\,\sigma$ = lead-time standard deviation
cov_L = lead-time coefficient of variation

$$E(w > w_o) = (1 - PF)Q/\sigma_L$$

To obtain w_o, gather the following measures from Table 10.1:
k = parameter associated with $c_T(k) = cov_L$
H(k) = probability of (z>k)
$\mu_T(k)$, $\sigma_T(k)$ = mean and standard deviation for parameter k of truncated normal
$\mu_P(k)$ = partial mean for parameter k
Also recall from Chap. 10, the following:

$$\begin{aligned} E(w > w_o) &= E(t > t_o)/\sigma_T(k) \\ &= E(z > z_o)/[H(k)\,\sigma_T(k)] \end{aligned}$$

Now compute the following:

$$E(z > z_o) = E(w > w_o)[H(k)\sigma_T(k)]$$

From E(z>z_o), use Table 10.1 to find z_o, and then compute w_o as follows:

$$w_o = [z_o - k - \mu_T(k)]/\sigma_T(k)$$

Finally, the safety stock becomes,

$$SS = w_o \sigma_L$$

Example 11.4 Suppose an item with the average monthly forecast of F=10, the standard deviation is σ=6, the lead-time is L=1 month, and the order quantity is Q=10 pieces. Use the percent fill method with PF=0.95, and the truncated normal distribution to find the safety stock.

The partial expectation for the item is computed as below:

$$\begin{aligned} E(w > w_o) &= (1 - PF)Q/\sigma_L \\ &= (1 - 0.95)10/6 \\ &= 0.083 \end{aligned}$$

Note the lead-time forecast is $F_L=10$, the lead-time standard deviation is $\sigma_L=6$, and the lead-time coefficient of variation is $cov_L=c_T(k)=0.60$. From Table 10.1, at $c_T(k)=0.6$, the truncated mean and standard deviation are approximately $\mu_T(k)=1.352$ and $\sigma_T(k)=0.812$, respectively. Further from the table, the truncated location parameter is $k=-1.1$ and $H(-1.1)=0.864$.

The corresponding value, $E(z>z_o)$ is obtained as below,

$$
\begin{aligned}
E(z > z_o) &= E(w > w_o)H(-1.1)\sigma_T(-1.1) \\
&= 0.083 \times 0.864 \times 0.812 \\
&= 0.058
\end{aligned}
$$

From Table 10.1, $z_o \approx 1.18$ corresponds to $E(z>z_o)=0.058$.

The value of w_o that conforms with z_o is computed below.

$$
\begin{aligned}
w_o &= [z_o - k - \mu_T(k)]/\sigma_T(k) \\
&= [1.18 + 1.1 - 1.352]/0.812 \\
&= 1.14
\end{aligned}
$$

Finally, the safety stock for the part is,

$$
\begin{aligned}
SS &= w_o \sigma_L \\
&= 1.14 \times 6 \\
&= 6.84
\end{aligned}
$$

In comparison when the normal distribution is applied with $E(z>k)=0.083$, the safety factor becomes $k=1.00$ via Table 10.1. The safety stock to use is computed below:

$$
\begin{aligned}
SS &= 1.00 \times 6 \\
&= 6.00
\end{aligned}
$$

As stated earlier, the truncated safety stock will be greater or equal to the counterpart normal safety stock.

In summary, the steps to compute the safety stock for the percent fill method from the truncated normal distribution are listed below:

1. From cov_L, get k, H(k), $\sigma_T(k)$ and $\mu_T(k)$ from Table 10.1.
2. Compute $E(w>w_o)$.
3. Compute $E(z>z_o)$.
4. Get z_o from Table 10.1.
5. Compute w_o.
6. $SS = w_o s_L$.

Summary

Safety stock is one of the most important measures in inventory control. The two common ways to measure the safety stock are the service level method and the percent fill method. Two probability distributions are described on how to determine the amount of safety stock needed, the standard normal distribution and the truncated normal distribution. No doubt, the standard normal is far more known and used. Although the truncated normal distribution is not known or used by most practitioners, it is the more appropriate distribution to apply when seeking the safety stock for each sku in the inventory. To use the normal distribution, when the truncated normal is appropriate, will result in a lower level of service (service level, percent fill), than is planned.

Chapter 12
Auxiliary Forecasts

12.1 Introduction

Management often needs forecasts unlike the models described in the earlier chapters that are generated using the flow of demands from the history months. This chapter describes some of the more commonly needed forecasts of this type. A first concerns the forecasts for the first future month and the demand-to-date as the month is progressing. For the first month, a forecast has already been generated, and as the month progresses, the demand-to-date demand is evolving. The forecast for the remaining portion of the month is generated along with the associated standard deviation. Another scenario occurs for parts when some demands are ordered for future deliveries, called advance demands. A forecast for the future month has already been generated in the usual way from the flow of history demands. An adjustment to the future month's forecast is developed based on the advance demand information. Another situation that often occurs in service parts inventory is when a forecast is needed on a part even when no history demands are available. This happens when a new part is included on the bill-of-material of a finished good item due to an engineering change or a redesign, and the part is to be immediately held in inventory at the service part location. This situation is called the initial buy quantity. Another condition that takes place often in service parts locations is when the supplier will stop supplying the part, even when the service part location is obliged to carry the part for future possible needs from its customers. This is called the all-time-buy.

12.2 Month-1 Forecasts and Demand-to-Date

Suppose a forecast system where the history demands, x(1), …, x(N), are used to generate the forecasts for the future months. The forecast for future month-1 is listed as x`(1), and the associated standard deviation is denoted as σ. Assume now

N. T. Thomopoulos, *Demand Forecasting for Inventory Control*,
DOI 10.1007/978-3-319-11976-2_12

where a portion, w, of future month-1 has elapsed and the demand to date is x_w. Note the forecast for this portion of month-1 would be,

$$F_w = w \times x`(1)$$

and the corresponding standard deviation is:

$$\sigma_w = \sqrt{w}\,\sigma$$

A compatibility measure that may be useful to the management is shown below:

$$k = \left(x_w - F_w\right)/\sigma_w$$

When all is in order, the accepted values of k are $(-3<k<3)$. In the event k is out of the range, the management may choose to review the forecast to make an adjustment. If $k<-3$, the forecast is too low, and if $k<3$, the forecast is too high.

The remainder portion of month-1 is (1-w), and the corresponding forecast and standard deviation are computed as below:

$$F_{(1-w)} = (1-w) \times x`(1)$$

$$\sigma_{(1-w)} = \sqrt{(1-w)}\sigma$$

The adjusted forecast for the total of month-1 becomes,

$$F'(1) = x_w + F_{(1-w)}$$

and the standard deviation is,

$$\sigma' = \sigma_{(1-w)}$$

Example 12.1 Suppose an item with the month-1 forecast of $x`(1)=100$ and the standard deviation is $\sigma=30$. Assume, $w=0.20$ of the month has elapsed and the demand-to-date is $X_w = 10$ pieces. Note the forecast and standard deviation for the w portion of month-1 is as below:

$$F_w = 0.2 \times 100 = 20$$

$$\sigma_w = \sqrt{0.20}30 = 13.42$$

The compatibility measure is:

$$k = (10 - 20)/13.42 = \text{-}0.745$$

and is well within the acceptable range of: $(-3<k<3)$.

The remaining portion of month-1 is $(1\text{-w})=(1-0.20)=0.80$. The associated forecast and standard deviation are:

$$F_{(1-w)} = 0.8 \times 100 = 80$$

$$\sigma_{(1-w)} = \sqrt{0.8} \times 30$$
$$= 26.83$$

For the total of month-1, the forecast and the standard deviation are as below,

$$F'(1) = x_w + F_{(1-w)}$$
$$= 10 + 80$$
$$= 90$$

and

$$\sigma' = \sigma_{(1-w)}$$
$$= 26.83$$

12.3 Advance Demand

On some occasions a demand for an item is known one or more months prior to the date the customer wants possession of the item. This is known as an advance demand. For example, in June, the customer orders the quantity prior to its need in August. The demand is part of the regular demand in August and not an addition to it. The forecast for the future months are already generated from the flow of demands of the past and with this extra advance demand knowledge, an adjustment to the forecast is applied.

Assume the current month is $t=N$ and $F(\tau)$=forecast for the τ th future month with σ the corresponding standard deviation. Further, let x_o=advance demand for future month τ. Of need now is an adjustment to the forecast for the τ th future month. It is assumed the demand for the future month comes from the normal distribution with parameters, $F(\tau)$ and σ. Note where,

$$k = [x_o - F(\tau)]/\sigma$$

and recall from Chap. 10, the partial expectation of the standard normal where $(z>k)$ is:

$$\mu_P(k) = E(z > k)$$
$$= \int_k^\infty (z-k) f(z) dz$$

The corresponding partial expectation for the demand, x, is:

$$\begin{aligned} E(x > x_o) &= \int_{x_o}^{\infty} (x - x_o) f(x) dx \\ &= E(z > k)\sigma \end{aligned}$$

and the corresponding standard deviation becomes:

$$\sigma\,(x > x_o) = \sigma_p(\kappa)\sigma$$

Recall also, where $\sigma_p(k)$ is the partial standard deviation of (z>k).

The forecast adjustment for future month τ becomes,

$$x_a(\tau) = x_o + E(z > k)\sigma$$

and the corresponding standard deviation is $\sigma(x > x_o)$.

Example 12.2 Suppose a part where the forecast for future month τ is $F(\tau) = 100$ and the standard deviation is $\sigma = 30$. Assume also an advance demand comes in for $x_o = 80$ pieces, and an adjustment to the forecast is needed. In this scenario,

$$\begin{aligned} k &= [80 - 100]/30 \\ &= -0.67 \end{aligned}$$

and with interpolation, Table 10.2 gives the partial expectation and standard deviation as, $\mu_P(-0.67) = E(z > -0.67) \approx 0.83$ and $\sigma_p(-0.67) \approx 0.79$, respectively. Thereby, the adjusted forecast is,

$$\begin{aligned} x_a(\tau) &= x_o + E(z > -0.67)\sigma \\ &= 80 + 0.83 \times 30 \\ &= 104.9 \end{aligned}$$

and the adjusted standard deviation is,

$$\begin{aligned} \sigma'(\tau) &= \sigma_p(-0.67) \times \sigma \\ &= 0.79 \times 30 \\ &= 23.7 \end{aligned}$$

Note in this example, the forecast goes up and the standard deviation goes down.

Example 12.3 Consider the same part as Example 12.2, ($F(\tau) = 100$, $\sigma = 30$), but now assume the advance demand is $x_o = 10$. In this scenario,

$$\begin{aligned} k &= [10 - 100]/30 \\ &= -3.00 \end{aligned}$$

and from Table 10.2, $\mu_P(-3.00)=3.00$ and $\sigma_P(-3.00)=1.00$. Thereby, the adjusted forecast is,

$$\begin{aligned} x_a(\tau) &= x_o + \mu_P(-3.00)\sigma \\ &= 10 + 3.00 \times 30 \\ &= 100.0 \end{aligned}$$

and the standard deviation is,

$$\begin{aligned} \sigma(\tau) &= \sigma_P(-3.00) \times \sigma \\ &= 1.00 \times 30 \\ &= 30.0 \end{aligned}$$

Note, there is no change in the forecast and standard deviation since the demand is at or below the range of minus three standard deviations.

Example 12.4 Suppose once more the same part as Example 12.2, ($F(\tau)=100$, $\sigma=30$), where now the advance demand is $x_o=190$ pieces. In this scenario,

$$\begin{aligned} k &= [190 - 100]/30 \\ &= 3.00 \end{aligned}$$

and Table 10.2 gives, $\mu_P(3.00)=0.00$ ανδ $\sigma_p(3.00)=0.00$. The adjusted forecast now becomes,

$$\begin{aligned} x_a(\tau) &= x_o + \mu_P(3.00)\sigma \\ &= 190 + 0.00 \times 30 \\ &= 190.0 \end{aligned}$$

and the standard deviation is,

$$\begin{aligned} \sigma'(\tau) &= \sigma_p(3.00) \times \sigma \\ &= 0.0030 \\ &= 0.0 \end{aligned}$$

Note when the advance demand is three or more standard errors above the forecast, $F(\tau)$, the adjusted forecast is the same as the advance demand, x_o, and the standard deviation reduces to zero.

12.4 Initial Forecasts

An important mission of a service parts distribution center (spdc) is to stock the parts for the finished good items (fgi) that are currently or previously in the lineup of products of the original equipment manufacturer (oem). This includes all the parts that are included in the bill-of-material (bom) of the fgi's that are currently in production and for those that have been in production for the past years. The oem is obliged to carry the parts for any maintenance or repair need by the customers for a fixed number of years after the part is no longer in the production of the fgi's on the assembly line. This length of time is called the obligation period.

At the beginning, when a new part is introduced in the bill-of-material for the fgi, due to an engineering or model change, the part must be stocked in the distribution center to fill any demands for the service and maintenance of the unit. A difficulty occurs in determining how much stock to buy since there is no demand history to base the buy decision. The first buy quantity on the part is called the initial buy quantity. The initial buy quantity requires an initial forecast of the part; one that is developed even when no demand history is available for the part. This situation is common for service parts where the parts are stored in a distribution center awaiting the demands from customers. The stocking location is confronted with determining how much to buy and store for each new part of this type. To accomplish, an initial forecast is needed.

The problem on how much to stock is indeed a very elusive and difficult one since there is no data to base the stocking decision. Often the decision on the amount to stock is assigned to experts who review each new part and determine the quantity to buy. The experts have little if any data to back their decisions and rely mainly on their experience.

The notions of new-parts-of-the-past (npop) and new-parts-of the-future (npof) are introduced. The npof are the parts where a forecast is needed now. The npop are the parts that have already occurred and where demand data is still available on the database for the initial year of their introduction.

An important element on the parts is here called an attribute (A), it describes the use of the part on the fgi. This could be a spring that is used on a door system, where each fgi has such a part. When possible, the attribute categorizes the type of part, its function, where it is used and so forth. The classification of attributes becomes valuable information to include on the database for each part.

For each npop, the average of the first 12 months of demand history is captured from the demand history. For a npof with an attribute A, all the npop with the same attribute are gathered and the first 12 months of their history demands are listed as D(i) where i identifies the i-th npop and n is the number of such parts. Hence, the data available becomes, D(1) ,…, D(n). Each yearly demand is now converted to a monthly average as d(i) = D(i)/12 for i = 1 to n.

From the monthly average demand history data, the average and variance of the demands are computed as shown below,

$$\mu_d = \sum_i^n d(i)/n$$

$$\sigma_d^2 = \sum_i^n \left[d(i) - \bar{d}\right]^2 / (n-1)$$

Because of the possibility of a large spread in the npop demands, the lognormal distribution (LN) is assumed for the parts. Thereby, d ~ LN(μ_y, σ_y^2) where y = lognormal of d, y = ln(d), with μ_y the mean and σ_y^2 the variance. Note the parameters of y are used as the parameters of d. The mean and variance of y are computed as below:

$$\mu_y = \ln\left[\mu_d^2 / \left(\sigma_d^2 + \mu_d^2\right)^{0.5}\right]$$

$$\sigma_y^2 = \ln\left[\left(\sigma_d^2 + \mu_d^2\right)/\mu_d^2\right]$$

The distribution of y is normally distributed whereby y ~ N(μ_y, σ_y^2).

It is possible now to select a group of probabilities where the values of y may occur. For convenience here, ten probabilities are selected as: (0.05, 0.15, …, 0.95.) For each of these, the associated value of the z value from the standard normal distribution is gathered and labeled as: [z(1), z(2), …, z(10)]. These become:

$$[-1.645, -1.036, -0.674, -0.375, -0.124, 0.124, 0.375, 0.674, 1.036, 1.645]$$

So now, ten values of y can be calculated by y(i) = [μ_y + z(i) σ_y] for i = 1–10. Each of the ten values are chosen to represent the center of a range with probability of 0.10. The corresponding values of d, are now computed by,

$$d`(i) = e^{y(i)} \quad i = 1 \text{ to } 10$$

Example 12.5 Suppose an engineering change to a fgi and a new part is included for the first time. The fgi will be produced on the assembly line and will contain this new part. The spdc is obliged to order some of these parts for any pending demands from the dealers to satisfy the potential customers needs on maintenance and repair. The engineers classify the part with an attribute A. The spdc computer system scans their database files to find any parts with the same attribute, A, where the first 12 months of service part demands are still available. In the example, $n = 5$ such parts are found. The average monthly demands of the five parts are labeled as d(i) i = 1 to 5 and are listed below:

$$d(i) = 1.2, 0.8, 1.5, 2.1, 9.3$$

The average, variance and standard deviation of the demands are computed with results below:

$$\bar{d} = \mu_{d'} = 2.98$$

$$s_d^2 = \sigma_{d'}^2 = 12.707$$

$$s_d = \sigma_{d'} = 3.565$$

Table 12.1 Ten selected probabilities, α(i), with corresponding standard normal variables, z(i), associated values of y(i), and of the average monthly demand, d`(i)

i	α(i)	z(i)	y(i)	d`(i)
1	0.05	−1.645	−0.903	0.405
2	0.15	−1.036	−0.329	0.720
3	0.25	−0.674	0.013	1.013
4	0.35	−0.385	0.285	1.330
5	0.45	−0.124	0.531	1.701
6	0.55	0.124	0.765	2.148
7	0.65	0.385	1.011	2.747
8	0.75	0.674	1.283	3.608
9	0.85	1.036	1.624	5.074
10	0.95	1.645	2.198	9.008

Recall, the monthly demands are assumed to follow a lognormal distribution. The corresponding normal variable, y, is obtained by

$$y = \ln(d)$$

where ln = lognormal. The parameters of y are the mean, variance and standard deviation and are computed as shown earlier. The resulting values are listed below:

$$\mu_y = 0.648$$

$$\sigma_y^2 = 0.888$$

$$\sigma_y = 0.942$$

The range of possible values of d is obtained in the following way. Ten selected probability points are selected as: 0.05, 0.15 ,…, 0.95 and are listed in Table 12.1. For each probability entry, the corresponding standard normal variable, z(i), is found where P(z < z(i)) = α(i). So now, the selected values of y are measured by,

$$y(i) = 0.648 + z(i)0.942 \quad i = 1 \text{ to } 10$$

Finally, the ten selected values of the average monthly demands, d, are:

$$d`(i) = e^{y(i)} \quad i = 1 \text{ to } 10$$

The table shows the average monthly demands, d, ranges from 0.405 to 9.008. Some ranges of d with probability estimates are the following:

$$P(1.013 < d < 3.608) = 0.50$$

$$P(0.405 < d < 9.008) = 0.90$$

$$P(d < 9.008) = 0.95$$

and so forth.

12.5 All Time Forecasts

In the production of a finished-good-item (fgi), many parts and components are needed in the assembly process. Each part has a supplier that replenishes the plant in a steady manner. As time passes, the collection of parts for the fgi is ever changing due to engineering and model enhancements. From time-to-time, the parts are needed at the service parts distribution center who replenish the dealers as customers seek maintenance or repair on their fgi. As the fgi is sold to the public, the population of fgi's with the part will increase over time as long as the fgi is still in production. The increase will halt when the part is replaced on the fgi because of an engineering change or for a model change. From then on, the population of fgi decreases as the units age and slowly are being scrapped. Thereafter, the demands start approaching zero.

When the part is no longer in use in production on the fgi, and with the demands dwindling at the spdc, the supplier will eventually find it unprofitable to produce the part and will notify the spdc that it will soon stop as the supplier of the part. The spdc is still responsible to carry the part for an obligation period, could be 5–15 years, after the part is no longer included in the bom of the current fgi. The spdc must order a quantity one last time from the supplier to carry for this all time need. This buy is often called the all-time-requirement (ATR). A forecast of the demands over the obligation years is now needed by the spdc.

A possible way to generate the forecast is given here. The method seeks to estimate the shape of the population of fgi units that have the service part included. The assumption is that the demands of the service part in question will be somewhat in parallel to the population of fgi's that have the part included. The method described here uses five parameters: (1) j_o = the number of years after a unit is sold to a customer where the fgi is free of being scrapped. For example, $j_o = 2$ will state that most likely the fgi will not be scrapped within the first two years of use by the customers. (2) r = the probability that a unit (of the fgi) will be scrapped in a year's duration. This is for each year after j_o years. If r = 0.1, 90% of all units of the fgi will continue to be used by the customer for yet another year, and 10% will be scrapped. (3) t_o = the number of years the part has been included in the bom of the fgi. This parameter identifies how many units have been produced by the oem. (4) T = the current year relative to the year of introduction of the part in the fgi. If the part is first included in the bom of the fgi in the year 2005 and the current year is 2013, T = 9 represents the number of years since and including the introduction year from 2005–2013. (5) N = the number of past years where the annual demands are available. For example, if the annual demands for the prior four years are still available on the database, $N=4$.

In summary, the parameters of this forecasting method are listed below:

Parameters:

j_o = scrap free years
r = probability of scrap per year after j_o
t_o = production years
T = current year (after part is introduced)
N = number years of part demand history

The forecast model seeks to estimate the shape of the population of fgi units with the part that are still in use by the customers. This requires estimating the probability of a unit being scrapped each year. For a given unit, j=the number of years after the customer has possession of the fgi unit, and p(j)=probability the unit is scrapped in year j is computed as below:

$$p(j) = 0 \qquad j = 1 \text{ to } j_o$$

$$= r(1-r)^{j-jo-1} \qquad j > j_o$$

The probability that the unit is scrapped in year j or sooner is noted as F(j), and the complement is H(j)=1—F(j). Note, H(j) is the probability the unit will not be scrapped by the customer in the first j years. In summary, these probabilities are below.

F(j)= probability the unit is scrapped in year j or sooner. [$F(j)=\sum_1^j p(j)$]
H(j)= probability the unit is not scrapped as of year j. [H(j)=1−F(j)]

For all the years after the part is introduced, the notation of t is used where $t \geq 1$. Of need here is to estimate the probability the fgi units will still be in use by the customers for t years after the introduction of the part. The summary of this notation is provided below assuming $t_o=4$ years of production:

t=number of years after part is introduced
H(1,t)= probability year 1 production unit is not scrapped as of year t
H(2,t)= probability year 2 production unit is not scrapped as of year t
H(3,t)= probability year 3 production unit is not scrapped as of year t
H(4,t)= probability year 4 production unit is not scrapped as of year t

The sum of the above probabilities by year, t, is used to estimate the shape of the population size that includes the service part in question. The notation uses x(t) to represent the sum of the probabilities as listed below:

$$x(t) = H(1,t) + H(2,t) + H(3,t) + H(4,t)$$

=generic shape of population in year t after introduction

The computation of x(t) is tallied for all the years from t=1 to T; the years from introduction to the current year.

From the database, the demands at the spdc for the N prior years are now gathered and listed as d(t), where,

d(t)=demand in year t for each year the service part demand is known.

For each of the N years where d(t) is available, the associated x(t) measures are gathered and the ratio of d over x is noted as dx and computed as below:

$$dx = \Sigma d(t)/\Sigma x(t)$$

=ratio of demand over generic shape where the sum is over the N demand years

Finally, the forecast of the service demands for the future years can be generated. The forecast for year t is denoted as f(t) and is calculated as follows:

$$f(t) = x(t) \times dx$$

Note, f(t)=forecast of the service part demand in year t for t>T

Example 12.6 Suppose the supplier of a part in the spdc informs the part will be dropped and requests one last time buy. The spdc is obliged to generate a forecast for the future years of the service obligation on this part. Assume the parameter values are below:

Parameters:

$j_o=2$= scrap free years
r=0.1= probability of scrap per year after j_o
$t_o=4$= production years
T=6= current year (after part is introduced)
N=4= number years of service part demand history

A first set of computations concern the probability the part will be scrapped in the j-th year after the customer takes possession of the unit. The probabilities, p(j), F(j) and H(j) are listed in Table 12.2. Note, for example, at j=4, p(4)=0.09, F(4)=0.190 and H(4)=0.810. Figure 12.1 is a plot of the flow of H(j) for twenty years after the unit of the fgi is sold to the customer.

Table 12.3 is a worksheet that yields the forecasts for the future years on the service part. The table shows, H(1,t) as the probability that a unit produced in year t=1 is still in use at year t. In the same way, H(2,t), H(3,t) and H(4,t) are the corresponding probabilities the units produced in years t=2, 3 and 4 are still in use in year t. The sum of the four probabilities is x(t), that represents the shape of the units in the population that have the service part in the fgi. The service demands known for N=4 years, (t=3, 4, 5, 6) is listed as d(t). The sum of the four years of d(t) with corresponding x(t) are shown below:

$$\Sigma d(t) = 110 + 120 + 130 + 125 = 485$$

$$\Sigma x(t) = 2.900 + 3.710 + 3.439 + 3.095 = 13.144$$

Table 12.2 Years, j, with probability of scrap in the year, p(j), cumulative probability of scrap, F(j), and probability not scrap, H(j)

j	p(j)	F(j)	H(j)
1	0.000	0.000	1.000
2	0.000	0.000	1.000
3	0.100	0.100	0.900
4	0.090	0.190	0.810
5	0.081	0.271	0.729
6	0.073	0.344	0.656
7	0.066	0.410	0.590
8	0.059	0.469	0.531
9	0.053	0.522	0.478
10	0.048	0.570	0.430
11	0.043	0.613	0.387
12	0.039	0.651	0.349
13	0.035	0.686	0.314
14	0.031	0.718	0.282
15	0.028	0.746	0.254
16	0.025	0.771	0.229
17	0.023	0.794	0.206
18	0.021	0.815	0.185
19	0.019	0.833	0.167
20	0.017	0.850	0.150

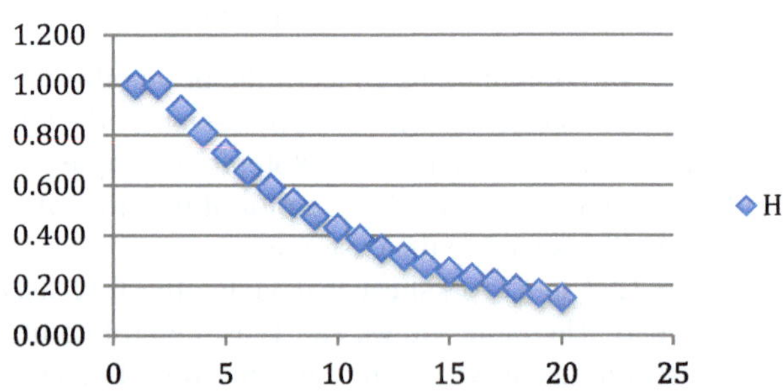

Fig. 12.1 Probability the unit is not scrapped as of year j, H(j), when the probability of scrap per year is r=0.1, and, scrap free years is $j_o=2$

So now, the ratio of d to x becomes

$$dx = 485/13.144 = 36.90$$

The forecasts for each of the years beyond T=6 are now calculated as,

$$f(t) = 36.90 \times x(t) \quad \text{for } t = 7 \text{ to } 20$$

Table 12.3 Years since introduction, t, probability of non-scrap, H(j, t), for production years j=1, 2, 3, 4, generic population of units, x(t), demand history, d(t), and annual forecasts, f(t)

t	H(1,t)	H(2,t)	H(3,t)	H(4,t)	x(t)	d(t)	f(t)
1	1.000				1.000		
2	1.000	1.000			2.000		
3	0.900	1.000	1.000		2.900	110	
4	0.810	0.900	1.000	1.000	3.710	120	
5	0.729	0.810	0.900	1.000	3.439	130	
6	0.656	0.729	0.810	0.900	3.095	125	
7	0.590	0.656	0.729	0.810	2.786		103
8	0.531	0.590	0.656	0.729	2.507		93
9	0.478	0.531	0.590	0.656	2.256		83
10	0.430	0.478	0.531	0.590	2.031		75
11	0.387	0.430	0.478	0.531	1.828		67
12	0.349	0.387	0.430	0.478	1.645		61
13	0.314	0.349	0.387	0.430	1.480		55
14	0.282	0.314	0.349	0.387	1.332		49
15	0.254	0.282	0.314	0.349	1.199		44
16	0.229	0.254	0.282	0.314	1.079		40
17	0.206	0.229	0.254	0.282	0.971		36
18	0.185	0.206	0.229	0.254	0.874		32
19	0.167	0.185	0.206	0.229	0.787		29
20	0.150	0.167	0.185	0.206	0.708		26

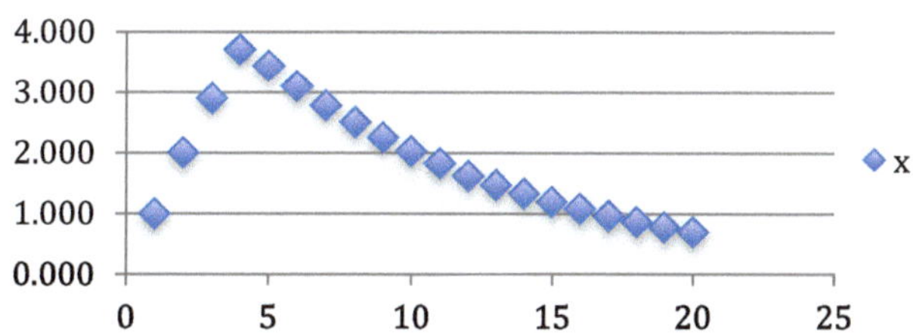

Fig. 12.2 Generic units in population in year t after introduction, x(t),

Note, for example,

$$f(7) = 36.90 \times 2.786 = 103$$

when probability of scrap per year is r=0.1, scrap free years is j_o=2, and production years is t_o=4 (Fig. 12.2)

Summary

Forecasts of the following type are described: (1) The month-1 forecast is adjusted as the month progresses and the demand-to-date becomes available. The forecast includes the remaining portion of the month-1 and the associated standard deviation. (2) Advance demand forecasts are needed when demands arrive months before the customer wants delivery. The advance demand forecast for a month is based on the flow of demands from the history months and also the advance demand for the future month. (3) In service parts, a forecast is often needed for a part that has no history demands. This occurs when the part is new on the bill-of-material, but yet the part is needed in stock at the service part holding location. (4) Also in service parts, a supplier may inform that the part will no longer be available and the service part location will need an all-time-buy. This requires a forecast on demands that may occur over the coming years for the obligation period of the part.

Bibliography

Abramowitz, M., & Stegun, I. A. (1964). *Handbook of mathematical functions with formulas, graphs, and tables*. (pp. 931–937). Washington D.C.: U.S. Department of Commerce.

Altay, N., & Lewis, A. (2011). *Service parts management: Demand forecasting and inventory control*. New York: Springer-Vertag.

Armstrong, J. S. (2001). *Principles of forecasting*. New York: Springer.

Brown, R. G. (1956). *Exponential smoothing for predicting demand*. ORSA, Nov.

Brown, R. G. (1959). *Statistical forecasting for inventory control*. New York: McGraw Hill.

Brown, R. G. (1962). *Smoothing, forecasting and prediction of discrete time series*. Englewood Cliffs: Prentice Hall.

Chase, C. W. (2013). *Demand driven forecasting*. New York: Wiley & SAS Business Series.

Chatfield, C. (2000). *Time series forecasting*. Little-John85, London.

Chisholm, R. K., & Whitaker, G. R. (1971). *Forecasting methods*. Homewood: Irwin.

Gross, C. W., & Peterson, R. T. (1976). *Business forecasting*. Boston: Houghton.

Hastings, C. Jr. (1955). *Approximation for digital computers*. Princeton University Press, Princeton, New Jersey.

Holt, C. C. (1957). *Forecasting seasonal and trends by exponentially weighted moving averages*. Pittsburg: Carnegie Institute of Technology.

Holt, C. C., Modigliani, F., Muth, J. F., & Simon, H. A. (1960). *Planning production inventories and work force*. Englewood Cliffs: Prentice Hall.

Hong, W. C. (2013). *Intelligent energy demand forecasting*. New York: Springer-Vertag.

Lewis, C. (1997). *Demand forecasting and inventory control*. New York: Wiley.

Mahaso, A. (2012). *Demand forecasting and management practices*. Zimbabwe: Lap Lambert Academic.

Makridakis, S., & Wheelwright, S. C. (1977). *Interactive forecasting*. San Franisco: Holden-Day.

Montgomery, D. C., & Johnson, L. A. (1976). *Forecasting and time series analysis*. New York: McGraw Hill.

Montgomery, D. C., Jennings, C. L., & Kulahci, M. (2008). *Introduction to time series analysis and forecasting*. New York: Wiley.

Moon, M. A. (2013). *Demand and supply integration*. Upper Saddle: F. T. Press.

Thomopoulos, N. T. (1980). *Applied forecasting methods*. Englewood Cliffs: Prentice Hall.

Winters, P. R. (1960). Forecasting sales by exponentially weighted moving averages. *Management Science*. Vol. 3, pp. 324–342.

N. T. Thomopoulos, *Demand Forecasting for Inventory Control*,
DOI 10.1007/978-3-319-11976-2

Index

N. T. Thomopoulos, *Demand Forecasting for Inventory Control*,
DOI 10.1007/978-3-319-11976-2

MIX
Papier aus verantwortungsvollen Quellen
Paper from responsible sources
FSC® C105338

If you have any concerns about our products,
you can contact us on
ProductSafety@springernature.com

In case Publisher is established outside the EU,
the EU authorized representative is:
Springer Nature Customer Service Center GmbH
Europaplatz 3, 69115 Heidelberg, Germany

Printed by Libri Plureos GmbH
in Hamburg, Germany